Culture Contact in Southern Mediterranean France

7th to 2nd Centuries BC

Daryn Reyman

BAR International Series 2076
2010

Published in 2016 by
BAR Publishing, Oxford

BAR International Series 2076

Culture Contact in Southern Mediterranean France

ISBN 978 1 4073 0637 7

© D Reyman and the Publisher 2010

The author's moral rights under the 1988 UK Copyright,
Designs and Patents Act are hereby expressly asserted.

All rights reserved. No part of this work may be copied, reproduced, stored,
sold, distributed, scanned, saved in any form of digital format or transmitted
in any form digitally, without the written permission of the Publisher.

BAR Publishing is the trading name of British Archaeological Reports (Oxford) Ltd.
British Archaeological Reports was first incorporated in 1974 to publish the BAR
Series, International and British. In 1992 Hadrian Books Ltd became part of the BAR
group. This volume was originally published by Archaeopress in conjunction with
British Archaeological Reports (Oxford) Ltd / Hadrian Books Ltd, the Series principal
publisher, in 2010. This present volume is published by BAR Publishing, 2016.

Printed in England

BAR titles are available from:

        BAR Publishing
        122 Banbury Rd, Oxford, OX2 7BP, UK
EMAIL   info@barpublishing.com
PHONE +44 (0)1865 310431
FAX   +44 (0)1865 316916
        www.barpublishing.com

Acknowledgements

The research presented in the following pages could not have been carried out or completed without the help of numerous individuals and institutions. Foremost among these are Professors Andrew Poulter and Lloyd Laing, who not only supervised the original dissertation work, but provided invaluable advice, support, help, and encouragement throughout the duration of my course.

I would also like to thank Professors Daphne Briggs, Anne Roth-Congés, D.W. Harding, Otto-Herman Frey, A. Trevor Hodge, and Peter Wells for their suggestions and permission to reproduce their figures, and Lloyd Laing for his illustrations.

And a final thanks to my parents, Arlene and Peter Reyman, my sister, Audra Reyman Wilder, my neice, Jayden Wilder, and my friends, Heather White, Christine Regalla, and Alex Schwendeman, whose love and support was only ever a phone call away.

Table of Content

Acknowledgments   i

Chapter 1
Hellenism and the Greek Colonization of Southern Gaul   1

  1.1 Hellenisation and Gallic Identity   1
  1.2 Greek Massalia (Marseille)   1
  1.3 Massaliote Comptoirs   4
    1.3.1 Citharista   4
    1.3.2 Tauroeis   5
    1.3.3 Olbia   5
    1.3.4 Antipolis, Nikaia, and the Stoechades Insulae   6
    1.3.5 Theline and Rhodanousia   6
    1.3.6 Agathe   7
  1.4 Massaliote Influence   7
    1.4.1 Writing   7
    1.4.2 Coinage   8

Chapter 2
Trade   10

  2.1 Introduction   10
  2.2 Trade routes   10
  2.3 Exports   10
    2.3.1 Wine   10
    2.3.2 Tin   11
    2.3.3 Pottery and jewellery   12
    2.3.4 Slaves and other perishable goods   12
  2.4 Reasons for Celtic-Greek trade: Celtic imports?   13

Chapter 3
Gallo-Greek Relations, Seventh Century – Fifth Century BC   15

  3.1 West central Europe, the Hallstatt Zone   15
    3.1.1 The Heuneberg   15
    3.1.2 Höhenapsberg   16
      Hochdorf   16
      Grafenbühl   19
      Klein Aspergle   20
    3.1.3 The Vix burial, Mont Lassois   21
  3.2 Celtic strongholds and Greek ports   23

Chapter 4
Consumption, Production and Southern Gaul   26

  4.1 Massaliote Influence in southern Gaul: the chora   26
  4.2 Indigenous Adoption   26
    4.2.1 Pottery   26
      Céramique claire   26

Grey-monochrome	27
4.2.2 Wine and Oil	27
Amphorae	27
Wine and Oil Production	28
4.3 Consumption, Production and Massalia	28
4.4 Implications for the role of Massalia	30

Chapter 5
Urbanism in Southern Gaul — 31

5.1 Late iron age culture	31
5.2 Iron age changes in hillfort and settlement construction	31
5.3 Changes in settlement patterns	32
5.4 Indigenous sites and urban development	33
5.4.1 Ensérune	33
5.4.2 Saint Blaise	34
5.4.3 Glanum	37
5.4.4 Entremont	40
5.5 The changing urban structure	42

Chapter 6
Art and Cult Sanctuaries — 45

6.1 Introduction	45
6.2 La Tène	45
6.3 Cult sites and sanctuaries	46
6.3.1 Entremont	46
6.3.2 Roquepertuse	48
6.3.3 Glanum	48
6.4 Religion	49
6.4.1 Representation of Celtic cults	50
6.5 Summary	53

Chapter 7
Overview of Gallic Relations with the Greek World — 54

7.1 Early Massaliote and Phocaean influence: trade and burial	54
7.2 Problems of assessing Hellenic influence on urban structure	54
7.2.1 The ordering of settlements: planning	55
7.3 Hellenic influence?	55
7.3.1 Celtic Influence in Massalia	56
7.4 Conclusion	56

References — 57

Abbreviations	57
References	57

Chapter 1
Hellenism and the Greek Colonization of Southern Gaul

1.1 Hellenisation and Gallic Identity

The archaeological record can produce, at most, an incomplete account of history. What is not preserved either archaeologically or historically is what composes the abstract fabric of society: belief systems, social organization and relationships, and certain aspects of the economy. As these generally cannot be extracted from the material record, they cannot be accurately reconstructed and it is best to avoid speculation. Inevitably, changes brought about by cultural interaction are defined and understood in different ways. Central themes, such as "Hellenisation," "Romanisation"[1] and "Gallic identity" must therefore be discussed before examining the interaction between the Gallic Celts and the Mediterranean world.

Like the archaeological and literary material, upon which the definitions of these terms are (necessarily) heavily based, they are open to different interpretations. At the most basic level, "hellenisation" is the expression of elements of Greek culture in territories outside Greece. These manifestations usually appear in the alteration of urban patterns and in the importation of foreign goods It is generally believed that these would have been accompanied by underlying changes in society and religious ideas and practices.

Unfortunately, this definition is more difficult than it may seem to apply to the archaeological evidence. It is archaeologically problematic. It is difficult to conclusively determine whether a society is hellenised or not: what is believed by one person to be definitive evidence may be seen as denoting something else entirely by another. This book is concerned with the Gallic Celts, a group of people which is difficult to define in terms of their material culture. As a result, identifying the changes in the outward manifestation of their culture is a tricky process. It is easy to forget what questions remain unanswered and this may lead to a biased interpretation. (see also chapter seven). For the time being, it is important to note that many of these questions are unresolved because of the lack of written sources and architectural expression, particularly in the case of religious structures. Changes that are observed must be ones which are easily recognisable. Examples of "Hellenic influence" on Gallic society include the orthogonal planning of settlements generally associated with the Greek poleis, the representation of Celtic cults, the importation of Mediterranean wine and the manufacture of wheel-turned pottery. In the material sense, changes evidently took place. Whether this was accompanied by a transformation in society is a much more difficult question to answer. The changing outward expression of a "culture" does not necessarily mean that society has changed internally.

Even so, it is by the presence or absence of material remains that we can make some attempt to define what is "Gallic" and what is "foreign." More often than not, Gallic identity can be defined by what is not as much as by what is; settlements contained no regular layout; most structures were not built in stone but in timber; the little art that was produced was two-dimensional and lacked realism; the fact that the Celts had no written language means that we are missing crucial information which could explain more about the character of their society. This also means we have an overarching problem - the inability to reconstruct Gallic social systems in any detail. The underlying beliefs that governed this society are not understood well enough to define Celtic identity.

Hellenisation did not completely replace the culture of the indigenous people. Elements of Greek civilisation were combined with those of the local culture in various ways. Consequently, judgements have to be made as to the degree to which Hellenism contributed to the creation of a new form of culture. Nevertheless, it is possible, as will be demonstrated below, to detect Celtic culture and its continued existence during the Hellenic period (sixth century BC through to the end of the second century BC). Similarly, just as the colonising Greeks exerted influence on the Gallic community, the Gallic community also exerted its own influence on the Greek settlers. The influence of the former is easier to detect, but a Celtic influence can be identified both within and around Massalia, notably in the production of ceramics and in the artistic representation (for further discussion see chapters 4 and 6).

1.2 Greek Massalia (Marseille)

The site of Massalia has been continuously occupied since its foundation by the Phocaeans in the sixth century (Dietler 1997, 282). A reconstruction of the ancient layout of the city is therefore difficult. However, limited excavations have yielded useful information, although sometimes scattered and incomplete (see Bouiron 1995; Conche 1996;

---

[1] Hellenisation and, especially, Romanisation, have been heavily debated. Numerous discussions have been published: Ebel 1976, 26-40; Mattingly 2007, 14-17; Millet 1990; Momigliano 1976; Wells 1980; Woolf 1997; 1998, 18.

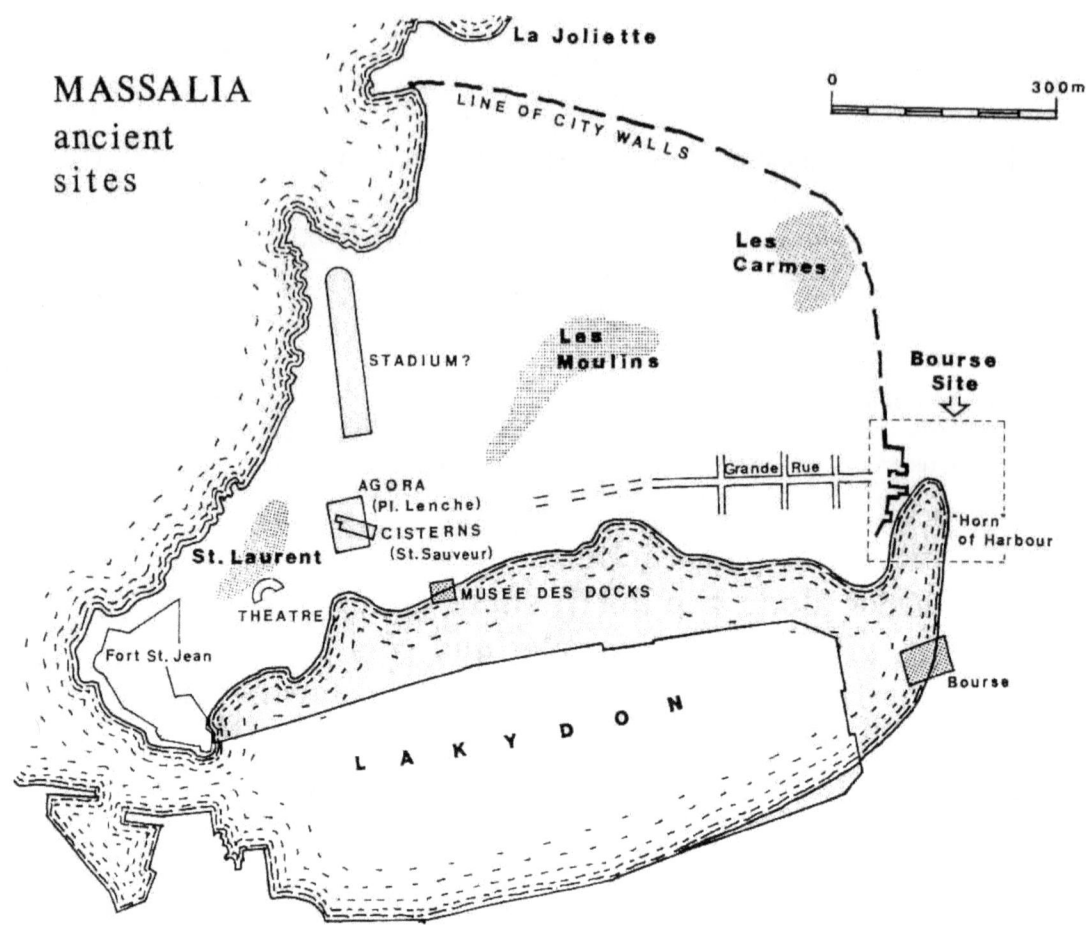

Figure 1.1: Greek Massalia (Hodge 1998, 77, fig. 51)

Gantès 1990, 1992a, 1992b; Gantès and Moliner 1990; Moliner 1996; Richarté et al 1995). This permits a partial understanding of particular aspects.

Massalia was situated on a rocky ledge, which was "washed by the sea on three sides" (Caesar Bella Civ. 1, 1), overlooking a small harbour (Figure 1.1). The ledge was connected to the mainland by an extension of the clay bedrock. This extension crossed a marshy area which was later furnished with a road determining the main axis of the city (Dietler 1997, 281; Euzennat 1980, 134). During the fifth century, there were several attempts to stabilise the road as is evidenced by pebbles, clay and a layer of empty amphorae (Bouiron 1995; Gantès 1992a, 75; Guery 1992; Euzennat 1980, 134). The road entered the city through a towered gate (Rivet 1988, 221).

Two partially superimposed fortifications were built. The older white rampart protected the landward side of the ancient city. It seems to have been initially constructed in the sixth century (Bonifay and Tréziny 1995), but has several later construction phases. The foundations are built of white limestone, quarried from nearby Saint-Victor, and were overlain by mud-brick (Dietler 1997, 281; Gantès 1990, 16; Arcelin and Tréziny 1990, 27). Although only found in discontinuous sections, the circuit is thought to have run from the Corne du Port (La Bourse) to the northern perimeter of La Butte des Carmes, terminating at a western point yet to be identified. During the third or second centuries, another wall, the "Wall of Crinas," was constructed (Figure 1.2). It can be traced for 200m on either side of its western gate. It was approximately 3m thick and constructed in emplekton technique. The pink facing stones were provided by a quarry located at La Couronne (Tréziny and Trousset 1992), and were decorated with herringbone patterns (discussed below, pgs. 56-57).

Although the initial Greek settlement is thought to have occupied only 12ha in the area of Fort Saint Jean (Vasseur 1914), Massalia rapidly expanded after its foundation (see Gantès 1992a). It had almost tripled in size by the mid-sixth century, encompassing 30ha and la Butte des Moulins. In the late sixth century, La Butte des Carmes and the Corne du Port (La Bourse) were also incorporated into the limits of the city and soon surrounded by a fortification wall (Hermary, Hesnard, and Tréziny 1999, 71). The settlement reached its greatest extent between the late fourth and second centuries BC, encompassing a total of 50ha (Gantès 1992a, 85; Tréziny 1995). At this size, Massalia was larger than most other settlements, indigenous or otherwise, in Mediterranean France. Conversely, it was small in comparison with Etruscan cities, the Greek colonies of southern Italy, or the northern and central late iron age oppida (Audouze and Büchsenschütz 1991; Collis 1984; Wells 1984).

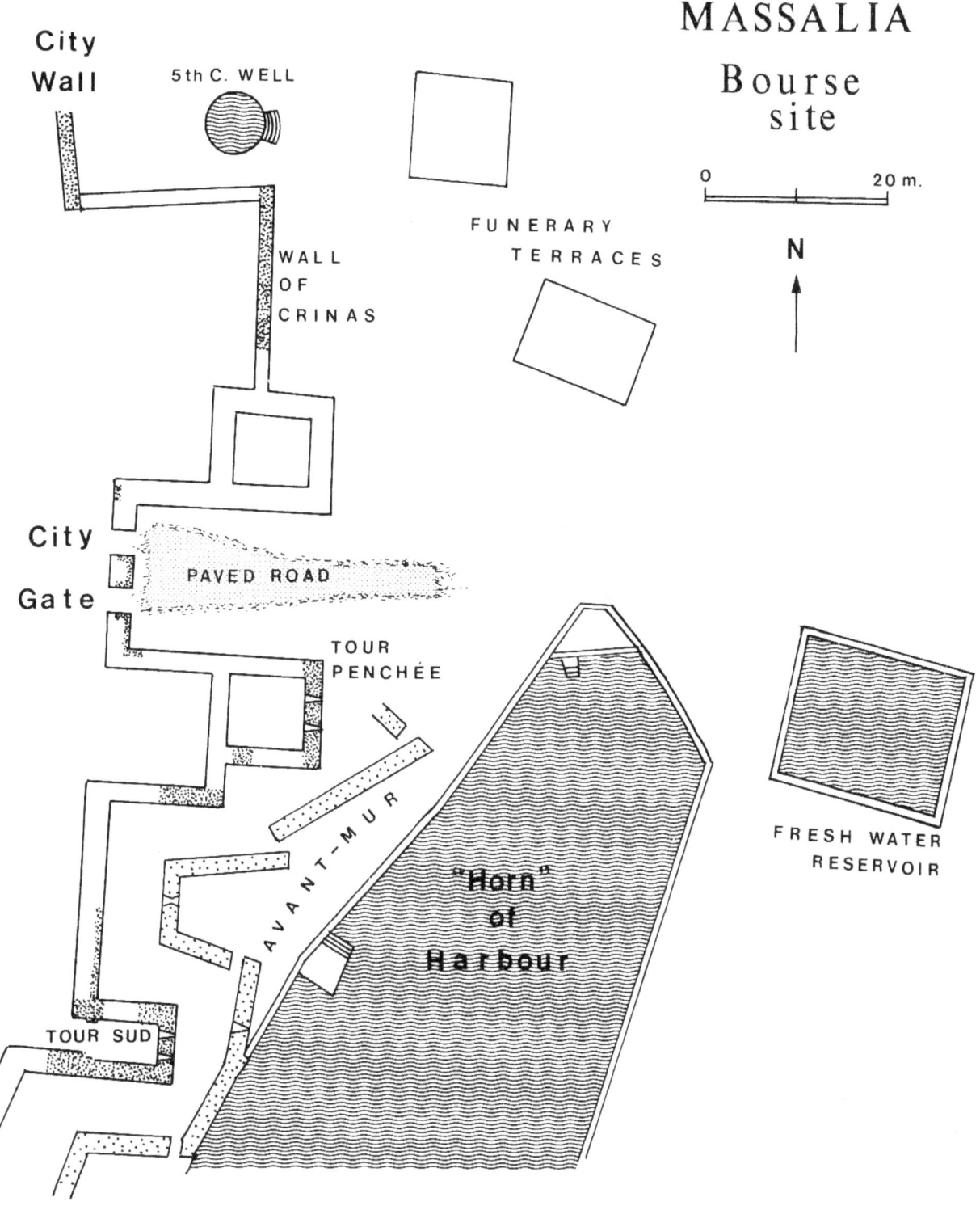

Figure 1.2: La Bourse site in Marseille (Hodge 1998, 81, fig. 53)

The rapid growth was accompanied by transformations in urban structure and a changing function of sites. This is best exemplified by the Rue Jean-François Leca (Hermary, Hesnard and Tréziny 1999, 73-79; Conche 1996), located at the base of La Butte des Moulins. In the late sixth to late fifth centuries BC, this area was used as a rubbish dump for the houses on top of the hill. By the mid-fifth century, it became an industrial site. It initially had a circular kiln for amphorae and a basin possibly used for clay preparation. This was later replaced by a structure containing evidence of bronze and iron working. A public bath complex supplanted the industrial site in the mid-fourth and late third centuries, and in the second century BC, a larger domestic building with an interior courtyard and workshop for metallurgy replaced the bathhouse.

Similarly, the port-side area of settlement was also continually changing (Heznard 1993; 1994; 1995). Recent studies have illustrated that progressive silting and relative changes in water level have drastically altered the shoreline since the first century BC (Arnaud and Morena 2004; Arnaud-Fassetta and Bourcier 1995; Morhange et al 1995; 1996; Gallia 1960, 286-290; Gallia 1962, 687; Tréziny 1995). At the time of its foundation, the bay of Massalia was much larger than it is today (Euzennat 1980, 134). Excavations at the Centre Bourse (see Bertucchi et al 1995; Bonifay and Tréziny 1995; Euzennat 1980, 1992; Guery 1992; Tréziny and Trousset 1992) and at the Place Jules Verne have examined various parts of the silted up harbour and port, demonstrating that the docks had to be continually reconstructed. Archaeological material from these sites range in date from the sixth century BC through to the late Roman and Medieval Periods. Likewise, organic material including nine wooden ships (Pomey and Heznard 1993), and wooden dock structures, cordage, baskets, leather, storehouses, and boardwalks was recovered at the Place Jules Verne. This indicates a continually changing occupation and function of the port-side areas; the port was composed of large stone blocks in the sixth century, the area was actively engaged in ship-building in the fourth, and the remains of hoists indicate that ships were being pulled into dry docks in the last two centuries BC (Dietler 1997, 282).

Funerary evidence from ancient Massalia is under-represented. As a result, there is insufficient data to generalise about funerary practices. However, seven cemeteries have been found (Morel 1995; Moliner 1994; Moliner et al 2004; Dietler 1997, 282-283; Euzennat 1980, 134; Hermary, Hesnard, and Tréziny 1999). All of these were located outside the city, proximal to postulated roads (see Moliner 1994).

1.3 Massaliote Comptoirs

Massalia began to establish daughter colonies, or "comptoirs," in southern Gaul as early as the sixth century BC (Figure 1.3). In general, the sites were founded relatively late and share certain characteristics. They are close to a body of water, indigenous settlements or, in some cases, on or near other important indigenous sites. Each of these characteristics facilitates importation, allows access to the indigenous community, and the development of trade. Their establishment is thought to have been primarily commercially motivated. There is also indication that these colonies were engaged in local production and the distribution of goods to both the indigenous population and each other (Reille 2001). Only the largest and most well researched sites are presented below, although several other Greek colonies may have existed (see Dominguez 2004).

It is interesting to note the chronological gap in the development of indigenous sites situated in the colonial hinterland of Olbia and Tauroeis (Bats 1990a, 175). Occupation on the settlements of Leobe, Castellas de Sollies in the Gapeau valley, Mont Garou, and La Courtine is attested from the sixth century BC until the beginning of the fourth century BC. The site is abandoned following the foundation of the Massaliote colonies. It is only at the end of the second century, that the settlements, once again, begin to develop urban character. Similarly, the sites of Florensac and La Monédière, near Agathe, were abandoned in the fifth century. Bigger cemeteries, like Mailhac, Coufflens and, slightly later, Pézenas are less used. Bérard, Nickels and Schwaller (1990, 184) suggest that these chronological disruptions may indicate the "expression of" colonial "control over its hinterland."

1.3.1 Citharista

Citharista (La Ciotat) was located just east of Massalia. It was situated just inside Bec de l'Aigle, a point of land protected by heavy seas. There is little more than a few Massaliote coins to indicate establishment prior to the fourth century. Several shipwrecks are located just off the coast, one of which was carrying Massaliote amphorae dated to the fourth century. There are, however, substantial roman remains of the late Republic and early Empire (Ebel 1976, 27).

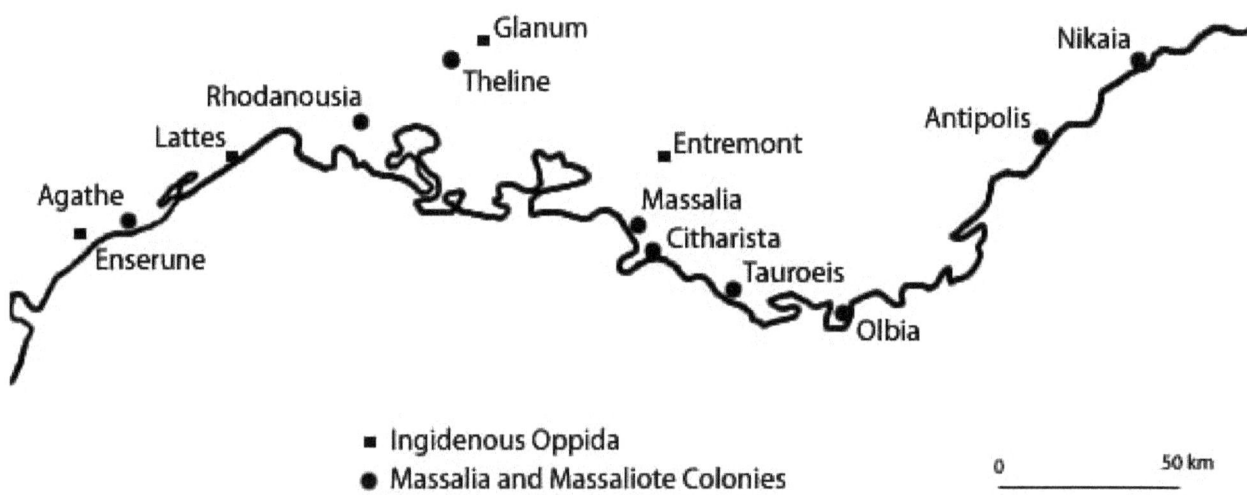

Figure 1.3: Map showing Massalia, Massaliote colonies, and several key indigenous settlements

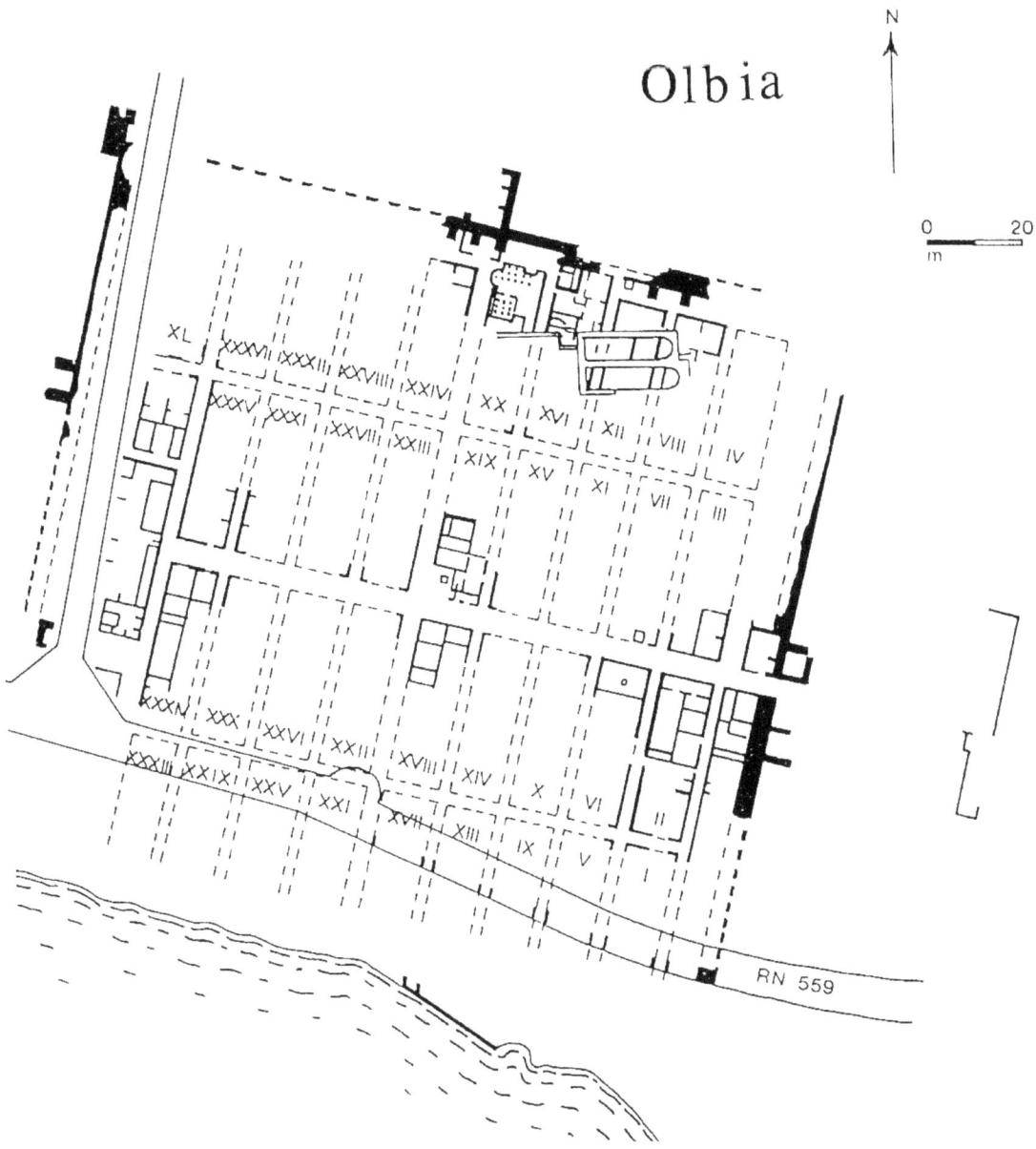

Figure 1.4: Olbia settlement plan (Hodge 1998, 175, fig. 96)

1.3.2 Tauroeis

Tauroeis is listed in ancient literary sources as a Massaliote colony (Strabo 4.1.5, 9; Caesar Bella Civ. 2.4.5, 149; Stephen of Byzantium v. 608.6). According to these sources, it was located twenty miles from Citharista, on the western side of Cap Sicie. Unfortunately, the exact location of the site is not assuredly known. While Greek artefacts have been found at several sites, the best argument places Tauroeis at Brusc (Duprat 1936; Layat 1959). Numerous Massaliote coins were recovered as were the remains of a Hellenic enclosure. The site was established between the late third and early second centuries (Brien-Poitevin 1990, 203-205) and occupied until the second century AD.

Regardless of the exact location of Tauroeis, it becomes evident that the placement of a site on the Cap Sicie would be highly beneficial to a society based on commerce. The Massif des Maures is close and mineral rich and several indigenous settlements were located in the hinterland. Mont Garou (sixth to fourth century BC) and la Courtine d'Ollouilles (fourth century BC), for instance, were well established by the time Tauroeis was founded.

1.3.3 Olbia

Olbia was founded around 330 BC near Hyères (Bats 1990b, 206; Bats 2006, 14; Morel 1995, 52, no. 62). Although now located on a peninsula, during ancient times, the site would have been separated from the mainland by water, corroborating the geography given by Strabo (4.15). Olbia was initially founded as a military defence against the hostile Saluvii. It was surrounded by several pre-colonial indigenous settlements, including the oppidum of Costebelle, occupied from the end of the sixth century to the beginning of the fourth century BC (Bats 1990a, 175).

Although construction during the Roman and Medieval Periods destroyed much of the Greek city, the archaeological remains of several Hellenic buildings have been uncovered (Figure 1.4). These include the sanctuary of Aphrodite, ramparts, and two habitation layers dating to the fourth and second centuries BC (Gallia 1962, 699). The sanctuary was built of large blocks, one of which bore the inscription, "Aphrodite." Two hundred ceramic cups and one hundred bronze Massaliote coins dating to the end of the third century were also found. The sanctuary was situated against the rampart, serving a double function as the northern wall. Another wall, constructed using different techniques, was later added doubling the fortification along this side (Bats 2006, 19).

Detailed studies of ceramic assemblages found at Olbia (Bats 1988a) have demonstrated a wide range of imported wares including Campainian, Massaliote, Attic, Italian and locally produced ceramics. Other imports have also been studied. A study by Rielle (2001) has shown that grindstones imported into Olbia were both exported to the indigenous populations and traded between Massaliote colonies.

1.3.4 Antipolis, Nikaia, and the Stoechades Insulae

Antipolis, Nikaia and the Stoechade Insulae (modern day Iles d'Hyères) were located close to the Alps. They were able to access the interior of the region via the Var valley.

Antipolis (Antibes) was divided into two sections: the acropolis, located on the plateau above the sea, and the harbour on the beach. The acropolis has yielded sixth and fifth century pottery, including Phocaean grey and banded pottery, Attic black-figure and red-figure ware, and various forms of Etruscan ceramics. Similarly, several shipwrecks have been found just off the coast. One of these was a fifth century Etruscan ship carrying Etruscan goods as well as Greek amphorae (Bouloumié 1990, 42-46; Long 2002, 25-31). Pottery assemblages found in the harbour are similar to those found in the acropolis.

As indicated by the archaeological evidence, the Massaliote colony of Antipolis was established very early (Pomp Mela 2.77; Strabo 4.1.5). This is in contrast to the majority of Massaliote comptoirs, which are generally of later date. Excavations have demonstrated, however, that the colony was not founded upon a virgin site. Indigenous occupation is attested from the tenth century onwards (Barruol 1969, 216; Bats 1990a, 175; Clergues 1969).

Across the bay from Antipolis was the easternmost colony of Nikaia (Nice) (Strabo 4.6.3). Unfortunately, the exact location of the colony is not known. Several finds indicate it may have been placed at the foot of the southern Alps, possibly near Rocher d'Antibes (Bats 1990a, 175). The fourth century artefacts include Attic coins, three pegs, and an inscribed bronze hand. Like Antibes, this could indicate Nikaia succeeded a pre-existing settlement, although, most scholars place Nikaia's foundation between 260 and 154 BC (Bats 1990a, 174-175; Bats and Mouchot 1990, 223). This is generally based on second century pottery finds from the cathedral of Notre-Dame-de-Chateau in Nice (Ducat and Farnoux 1976, 15-19; FOR I, no. 25-27; Gallia 1954, 441-442). The date of 154 BC is given as a terminus ante quem based on the knowledge that both Nikaia and Antipolis were besieged by the local population at this time.

Strabo (IV, 1, 5) and Tacitus (Hist. III, 43) attest to the Massaliote control of the set of islands called the Stoechades Insulae. Archaeological remains which lend support to this claim have been discovered on the islands of Giens and Porquerolles. Archaic shipwrecks, dating to 515 BC and 475 BC, have been discovered off the coast of Porquerolles (see Long, Miro, Volpe 1992), while on the island, remains of a first century town have been found (Brun 1992). On Giens, the remnants of a Greek shrine dedicated to Aristaeus and pottery dating between the second century BC and the first century AD were also recovered. Many of the pottery fragments bore Greek inscriptions, all of which were dedications to Aristaeus (Gallia 1975, 562; 1977, 501; 1979, 558-559; 1981, 537). Both islands have yielded vestiges of ports (FOR II, nos 44-45 and no. 47).

1.3.5 Theline and Rhodanousia

Until fairly recently, Theline and Rhodanousia were little more than names, roughly located around the Rhône.[2] Although identification is still conjectural, recent studies have identified two sites as potentially those of Theline and Rhodanousia (Bats 1990a, 174).

According to Festus Avienus (Ora Maritima, v. 689-691), Theline was located around the modern day city of Arles. Unlike the rest of these sites, ancient Arles was a relatively large site founded in the first half of the sixth century BC. The early settlement shows rapid expansion (Arcelin 1990, 196-198), especially after it was doubled in size by the construction of regular, rectangular insulae. Before c. 530, imported ceramics comprised only ten to twenty per cent of the pottery assemblage. After this time, ninety per cent of the ceramic material found was imported (Arcelin 1990, 198). These included Attic wares (Arcelin and Rouillard 2000; Rouillard 1992), banded pottery, and Massaliote amphorae (Sourisseau 1990). It has been suggested that this may indicate the annexation of Arles as a Massaliote comptoir (Bats 1990a, 174). After 375 BC, the situation changed. Indigenous ceramics double in quantity and non-turned pottery was locally manufactured and/or imported from other regions of western Provence (Arcelin 1990, 198). It is possible that this demonstrates the relinquishment of Massaliote control and a return to indigenous authority. This change, however, is not accompanied by any disruption in the archaeological record: there is no evidence of violence, burning, or destruction. Arcelin (1987) suggests that this may indicate an advanced, highly-pressured fourth century indigenous population. No cultural or economic disruption with Massalia would have been necessary; the founding city would have kept the settlement and its harbour in its sphere of influence as a certain degree of inter-dependence had already been established. Similar evidence has been found at Arles-Van Gogh, located several kilometres away (Morel 1995, no. 64).

Rhodanousia is proposed to have been located at Espeyran

---

[2] The identity of their founders is also debatable. Ancient sources suggest they could have either been Rhodian or Massaliote establishments. Festus Avienus *Ora Maritima*, v. 690-692; Strabo 3.160, 4.1.5, 4.1.6; Ps.-Scymnos v. 202-209; Stephen of Byzantium v. 542.15, 546.1.

(Barruol and Py 1978a, 94-100; Py 1990a, 191-192). This is a problematic association and recently, doubts have been expressed (Bats 1986, 41 and n.63; Py 1990b, 112-113, 284-285). Literary sources citing Rhodanousia are few, sometimes inaccurate, and generally only give topographical information concerning location (Ps-Scymnos v. 208, Stephen of Byzantium v. 542.15 and 546.1, Strabo 4.1.5). The archaeological evidence - post-holes and various signs of fire - date to the last quarter of the sixth century demonstrating the early use of the site. No architectural remains, however, appear in the record until 475 BC. These consist mainly of brick walls. Conversely, the ceramic assemblage is composed of a high percentage of Massaliote amphorae, and fine Massaliote vases. This is characteristically different from the assemblages of other sites in the Nîmes region and even those from the Massaliote colonies of Agde and Olbia (see Bats 1988a).

1.3.6 Agathe

Agathe (Agde) is located on the bottom of a hill on the Hérault, a short distance upstream from the coast. It has a quiet, defensible harbour, and was located exactly midway between Emporion and Massalia, and adjacent to a hinterland rich in minerals (Bats 1990a, 176). While ancient sources agree that it is the most westerly Massaliote colony (Pliny Nat Hist 3.5 and 33; Ps-Scymnus v. 208; Stephen of Byzantium s.v. Agathe; Strabo 4.1.5), they disagree as to whether it was originally a Rhodian or Massaliote foundation. Agathe was the only other colony established relatively early. The site was occupied in fifth century BC (Bérard, Nickels, Schwaller 1990, 184; Garcia and Marchand 1995; Nickels 1981; 1982; 1983, 422). Like several of the sites mentioned above, Agathe may have been initially aligned with an earlier indigenous settlement; Greek artefacts were found 20km away at La Monédière in Bessan, a settlement dating to the seventh century (Bats 1990a, 174-175).

Agathe was small, covering only 4ha. The city was divided in two by a platea. By the mid-fifth century BC, the site had been given an urban organisation. This was supplanted by four successive grid-like urban layouts (Nickels 1981, 30-31). At the mouth of the river, remnants of the rampart were discovered. The wall was constructed of mud-brick on top of basalt blocks. Between the fifth and second centuries BC, a land cadastre was emplaced, indicating the limits of the city and its external territory, as well as land allotment. Agathe is the only site from which an example of pre-Roman cadastration is known (Clavel-Lévêque 1982; Guy 1995; Benoit 1978).

Underwater archaeology of the river and the neighbouring sea has yielded material indicating an active sea trade (Bouscaras RSL XX 1954, 47-54). Among the evidence found were counterweights for presses (Garcia 1992b, 242-243) and ancient anchors. In addition, over 100 complete amphorae of Etruscan, Phocaean, Greek and Italian provenance were uncovered. They ranged in date from the sixth century BC to late Roman times. Many of these were still sealed, but only small traces of their contents were left; the majority was leached out by the sea.

There are several indigenous settlements to the north, Florensac, abandoned at the end of the fifth century, and Pézenas. Peyrou, a cemetery 500m outside Agathe, is situated on a small hill 12-14m high. All of these sites demonstrate early Mediterranean contact. Peyrou has several cups dating to the seventh century (Bérard, Nickels and Schwaller 1990, 183-184; Landes et al 2003, 168-197; Nickels 1989, 288-289; Nickels et al 1981, 90-125) and the indigenous settlements have imported Etruscan goods (Landes et al 2003, 169-182). Shipwrecks carrying Etruscan goods have also been found, one of which dates between the end of the seventh century and the first half of the sixth century (Garcia 2002, 40).

1.4 Massaliote Influence

1.4.1 Writing

There are many questions that are still unanswered in regard to the adoption of writing by the indigenous population. The process of this adoption, the degree of literacy and any association writing may have with social status is, as of yet, unknown. It is clear, however, that writing was adopted several centuries after Phocaean contact and the establishment of trade with both Massalia and Emporion[3] in Iberia. Although the majority of the examples are graffiti, generally names scratched onto various artefacts including ceramics (see Bats 1988b; 2004), other examples of writing do exist. For instance, stone and funerary inscriptions have been found (see Panosa Comingo 1993; Lambert 1992). Despite various contacts with the Mediterranean world (see chapter three), only two scripts became prominent in southern France: Greek and Iberian. Writing was not used by all southern Gallic populations. The Ligurians of the Cote d'Azur, for example, seem not to have adopted any writing system at all (Dietler 1997, 305).

The Greek alphabet was not adopted by the indigenous community until the third century BC, almost four hundred years after the foundation of Massalia. Use was generally confined to the Lower Rhône Basin and originally thought to have represented the Gallic language (Lambert 1992). Two abecedaries from Lattes, however, have recently provided evidence that the Greek language may have been used as more than just a means of writing (Bats 2004). It may have given rise to a new form of syncretism, Gallo-Greek. Similarly, the Iberian alphabet also began to be used by the southern Gallic people several centuries after its creation.[4] The earliest examples date to the mid-fourth century and use seems to be restricted to Western Languedoc and Roussillion (Bats 1988c; Dietler 1997, 305).

---

[3] Emporion was a Phocaean *poleis* established in Iberia around 600 BC (Dominguez 2004, 164). As will be demonstrated in the following chapters, Iberian and Greco-Iberian influence stemming from Emporion has a profound affect on Western Languedoc and Roussillion, regions of southern France in the closest proximity.

[4] Iberian script developed in Southern Spain during the seventh century BC as a representation of Phoenician writing (Dietler 1997, 305).

1.4.2 Coinage

Coinage was invented in the seventh century in the eastern Mediterranean (Grierson 1978) and quickly spread to other regions. By the sixth century, Massalia was minting its own coins (Blanchet 1905, 226-238; Brenot 1989; Furtwängler 1978), followed by two colonies located in Spain, Emporion in the fifth century, and Rhoda in the third (Dietler 1997, 304). Together with fourth coinage from Macedonia (Kellner 2000, 475-477), these issues provided the stimuli for Gallic tribal coin production.

When trying to reconstruct the southern Gallic indigenous adoption of the monetary system, it becomes evident that a detailed picture is lacking. Gallic tribes began to strike their own coinage in the third century BC. It is not until the second century, however, that a "quantitatively significant" amount of regional and individual site evidence is available for monetary circulation in Mediterranean France (Gentric 1981; Py 1990b, 600-607; Py 1993a, 255; Richard 1990; 1992; Richard and Villaronga 1973; Taffanel et al 1979). Coinage with a wide enough distribution and in large enough quantities is generally only found on large settlements dating to the first century BC and is probably largely attributable to Roman occupation. By this point Roman administration had governed the area for a generation; the province Gallia Narbonensis was annexed in 125 BC.

The initial reason why the Gauls adopted monetary systems has been widely discussed. Coins were probably initially valued for their metal. They would not have been used as a system of exchange, but hoarded, melted, and re-used. There is some evidence indicating that this may have been the case. First, Massaliote heavy drachmae, original Macedonian coins and their imitations are rarely found (Kellner 2000, 475). Second, little direct evidence of Greek coins in Celtic territory exists which attests to trade routes (Allen and Nash 1980, 3). Several Rhodian coins were overstruck with indigenous motifs (Allen and Nash 1980, 14), and an early hoard, dated to c. 500 BC, was found at Auriol (Furtwängler 1978; Pournod 1990, 146-153). Several other hoards have been found, all of which are considerably later than that of Auriol: La Courtine (Brenot 1989) and Emporion (Villaronga 1986, 49), deposited in the third century, and Entremont in the second (Congès 1990, 154). However, it must be said that hoards are only archaeologically useful in establishing the relative chronology of coins and must be viewed as exceptional circumstances. For the distribution of coinage, single finds are more useful (Allen and Nash 1980, 3-4). Furthermore, any finer detailed analysis of the adoption of the monetary system by the indigenous people needs a greater amount of archaeological support. Material evidence is scarce and it gives limited clues to its origin. The first issues seem to be outright imitations. As a result, it is impossible to locate the area where the first Celtic issues were made (Allen and Nash 1980, 3; Kellner 2000, 475-476). Only later were a greater variety produced, becoming more and more varied, and ultimately leading to localised varieties (Allen and Nash 1980, 3). This can best be exemplified by the Gallic imitations of Rhodian and Macedonian coins.

The foreign currencies from Rhoda and Macedonia were rapidly imitated after their introduction. Indigenous variants of these coins were attested in southern Gaul, as well as in central and northern regions (Allen and Nash 1980; Kellner 2000, 475-477). However, many are characterised by reduced silver content, and the transformation of original motifs into stylised Celtic representations. For instance, a Rhodian drachma bearing a four-leaf rose was imitated by the Tectosages (Kellner 2000, 476). The four-leaf rose became a cruciform pattern, with stylised leaves and various decorations adorning the fourth leaf. These spread north where they became a prototype for the cruciform coins in Germany and Noricum. Rhodian coins seem to have been very prominent in Languedoc and Roussillion. Conversely, Massaliote coins were dominant in Provence, although their distribution seems to have been confined to the lower Rhône Basin until the end of the third century (Dietler 1997, 304), contemporary with when some Gallic tribes began minting their own coinage. Gallic types include the monnaies à la croix of the Volcae Tectosages (situated between the Garonne and Loire), and the Neronenses coins found in large quantities at Montlaurès. The individual coin series of the former, bore legends in Greek, Iberian and Latin. The names of individual tribal leaders were also sometimes given (Allen and Nash 1980, 14, 55-6; Dietler 1997, 304-305).

Roman involvement in the area must also be addressed. Even before the annexation of southern Gaul as the province of Gallia Narbonensis, the Romans were actively involved in the area for various reasons (Clerc 1930, 1-26, 27-30; Clavel-Lévêque 1977, 132-166; Ebel 1976): transporting troops to Spain during the first and second Punic Wars, and quelling uprisings of indigenous people against Massalia. This is evidenced in the coinage. In the mid-to late third century BC, silver coins began circulating on each bank of the Rhône. These coins combined various Roman motifs and weights that were borrowed from Roman coinage in the first quarter of the next century. Those from the left bank later spread to eastern and central Gaul and beyond (Allen and Nash 1980, 15). Similarly, small bronze coinage found in Provence and Languedoc were relatively contemporaneous with the monnaies à la croix. These seem to have been issued by and for the Celtic people and indirectly derived, via Iberia, from the Roman system in the second century BC. Similarly, Massaliote issues of the third century adhered to the Roman weight system (Brenot 1990). After Narbonensis was annexed, Roman influence spread over increasing area.

Several scholars have said that the measure of Massalia's cultural and commercial influence in southern Gaul can be seen in the distribution of Massaliote coins (Colbert de Beaulieu and Richard 1970; Richard and Villaronga 1973, 81-131; Rolland 1935; Rolland 1949; Rolland 1960). Although there is limited evidence for Massaliote coin imitation,[5] the evidence from Celtic coins must also be taken into account. There is no indication that Celtic coinage was meant to function as a method of exchange. The local and regional differences in currencies demonstrate a wide range of weight conventions. This alone would probably provide problems in coin exchange with neighbouring Celtic tribes, let alone with established civilisations with major currencies, such as that of the Greeks and Etruscans. Furthermore, in general, series of coins have very narrow distributions. Studies done at Cayla de Mailhac, demonstrate that money before Augustus was supplied by the big settlements in the vicinity which ended up supplying secondary settlements with local and Roman issues (Taffanel et al 1979, 52). When the currencies did circulate outside the narrow distribution areas, there is no indication of a standardised exchange rate similar to that which exists today. Therefore, the price of a coin would have been subject to test and assay.

---

[5] See Taffanel et al 1979. Before 325 BC, only two types of coin were found at Cayla de Mailhac; an obol and a possible imitation of a Massaliote obol. Unfortunately, the stratigraphy of Mailhac does not seem to allow for precise dating. Most other coins were found in two layers each with a very wide range of dates: Cayla IV (325-75 BC) and Cayla V (75 BC – 200AD).

CHAPTER 2
TRADE

2.1 Introduction

Although the main region of concern is southern Gaul, it cannot be viewed in isolation. Much of its development is rooted in the early establishment of trade relations between Massalia and the Celtic strongholds situated in the north and central interior. This initial socio-economic contact introduced Mediterranean goods to indigenous society, thereby helping to create new cultures, such as La Tène (discussed below, pgs. 59-60), and beginning the process of "hellenisation." Even though regional differences do exist in terms of the contexts in which these foreign items are found, many of these imported products became incorporated into Gallic life and funerary practices. As a result, without a discussion of trade relationships a very one-sided view would be presented and it would be impossible to fully understand the later divergent development between north/central regions and southern Gaul.

2.2 Trade routes

Many attempts have been made to reconstruct and/or secure routes used to transport goods from Massalia into the interior of Gaul. While various hypotheses have been put forward, including overlapping paths in the eastern Alpine Passes (Kimmig 1958, 75-87), through the western Alps, and in the central Passes (Megaw 1966, 40), most of these are generalizations. The geography of Gaul, Italy and hinter Spain is complex, making only certain combinations of overland, river and sea routes really feasible. Likewise, it is important to note that trade routes cannot be known for certain, but only implied through the use of archaeological and literary evidence.

If traditional models, new ideas and finds, and the distribution patterns of various items are used collectively, it is possible to demonstrate the most travelled routes from one region to another.

None of these routes were used exclusively by one civilization or for the distribution of one particular type of item. On the contrary, one kind of good, ie attic black-figure ware cups, may have been transported by several different groups using various roads.

Most itineraries are therefore defined by the distribution of several types of widely circulated items such as amphorae and black bucchero ware. For instance, bucchero ware has been found in Massalia, the Midi, and along the southern coast of Iberia (Benoit 1965, 15-20). The interconnectivity of routes, however, is probably best illustrated by Etruscan and Massaliote wine, as well as the appearance of Mediterranean table and drinking services in Gaul.

It becomes obvious that river valleys were the most conducive to economic exchange and transportation. Not only would this location facilitate transport, but it would have enabled the population to exploit the rich soils. As a result, many of the Celtic settlements associated with wealthy burials (discussed in chapter 3) were situated near major rivers. Similarly, the important port colonies of Massalia, and later, Adria and Spina, were located on the deltas and mouths of major rivers such as the Rhône and Po. Because of this, many trade routes were probably focused on river transport and the associated overland routes which linked one river to another (see Figure 2.1). For example, the Rhône-Saône-Doubs could have been used to access the Seine, the Loire, and the Rhine.

2.3 Exports

2.3.1 Wine

There is evidence demonstrating that grape vine had grown in France since the Quaternary Period. However, local production of wine is not thought to have begun until after the foundation of Massalia[1] (Justin XLIII, 4.2). According to Athenaeus (IV, 152C), the Massaliotes exported wine to indigenous settlements, although it was rare (Martial X 36).

Graeco-Massaliote amphorae fragments were found at the Heuneberg. These fragments were found in association with an increased number of black-figure Greek vase shards, supporting the concurrent importation of Mediterranean dining services. Both of these types of items must been distributed via the route along the Rhône, Saône, and Doubs rivers (Figure 2.2). Overland routes would then have had to have been taken to transport the goods directly to the nearby hillforts, including those at Mont Lassois, and the Heuneberg.

Prior to the Massaliote exploitation of the Rhône, wine and other associated wares probably were transported along a north-south Alpine route. This is supported by two pieces of evidence. First, the distribution of imported Etruscan wine amphorae and high-quality wheel made pottery found at the

---

[1] For a discussion of local-production of wine, transport amphorae and distributions see below.

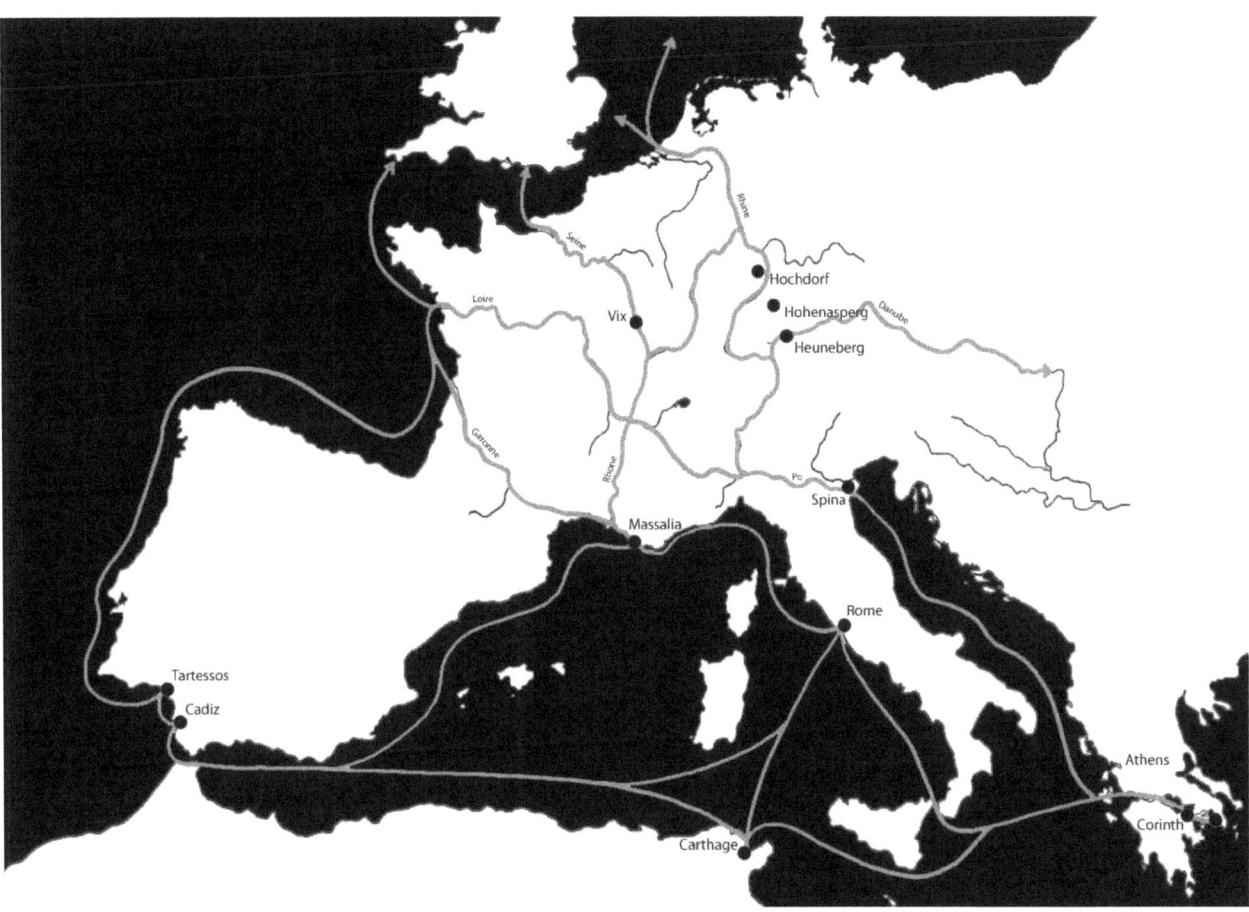

Figure 2.1: Proposed trade routes during the 6th century BC (After Haywood 2001, 51)

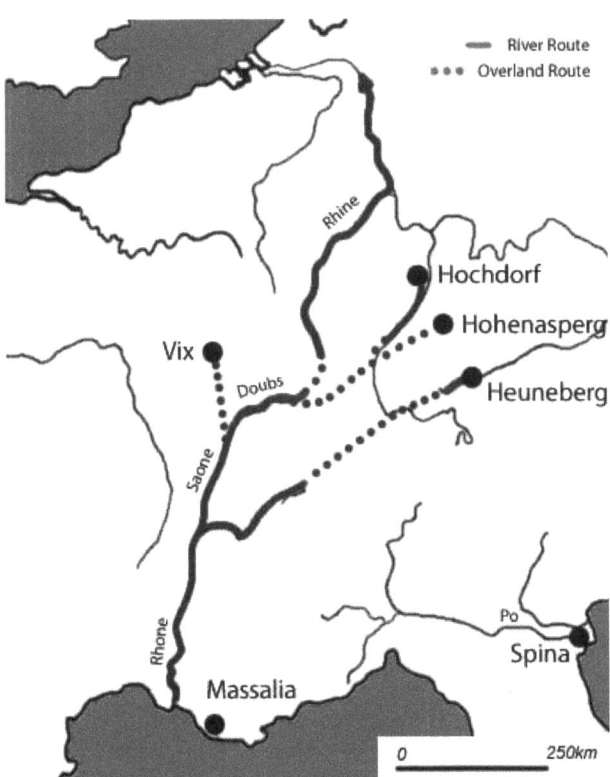

Figure 2.2: Proposed Rhone-Saone-Doubs-Rhine trade route and possible associated overland routes

Heuneberg suggests an Alpine route (Kimmig 1975, 44-46). Second, the forerunner to these ceramic wares originated in central Italy. The knowledge of these forms must therefore have been transmitted to the Heuneberg over the central Alpine passes based on geographic location.

2.3.2 Tin

Tin was not only essential for the production of bronze, but also an essential commodity exploited extensively during the late iron age. Although Strabo (iii, 5.11) describes tin from the Cassiterides, other sources of Atlantic tin existed. Cornwall in Britain was considered a source,[2] as were Armorica, Brittany, and Galicia (Penhallurick 1986, 85-104). Preliminary studies undertaken at the British Museum Research Laboratory have also raised the possibility that some tin may have come from Iberia. Unfortunately, the lead content was too insubstantial to merit a definite conclusion (Treister 1997, 155).

The participation of the Massaliotes in the British tin trade has long been debated. The discovery of Gallic imitations

---

[2] Cornwall has long been implicated in the tin trade as has foreign, particularly Phoenician, interest (Festus Avienus *Ora Maritima*, v. 113-115; Strabo iv, 2,1; iv, 5, 2). Mining waste from south-west England is so far unknown (Treister 1997, 154), but there is growing evidence for ancient tin working. See Pearce 1981, 126-127, 156-157; Penhallurick 1986, 123-131, 139-152, 173-224. Various literary sources also make reference to Cornish tin.

of Massaliote and Macedonian coins[3] in Britain have provided some evidence of cross-channel Gallic and Greek links. However, they must be considered with caution as provenance cannot always be ascertained (De Jersey 1999, 202-203 and note 3). Regardless, many scholars have proceeded with trade route studies under the assumption that Massalia was an active participant in the Cornish tin trade.

Originally, tin was thought to have travelled down the Rhône Valley, possibly via the Seine and Saône (Diodorus, v. 22), to Massalia. The simplicity of this model has been challenged by recent findings. Evidence suggests the transportation of goods from the Mediterranean along routes accessed from the Rhône. The route from Cornwall to the Rhône, via the Seine, conversely, remains doubtful (Graham, CAH iii/3 (second edition), 140f.). Atlantic tin was most likely "shuttled" along the coast of Gaul and exchanged with the Gallic peoples at various points, especially those situated on river estuaries (Cunliffe 2001, 302-306; Nash 2003, 245). It has been proposed that this was an old circuit linking Gaul and Italy long before Massalia was colonised. There is some evidence supporting this idea. For instance, many Villanovan and Etruscan artefacts dating between the ninth and sixth centuries BC have been found in western France between Languedoc and Armorica (Milcent 2002). Likewise, a bar ingot was found in Paris along with Navicella Italic fibuale, all of which was in an early Hallstatt context (Gran-Aymerich 1997, 203).

After the establishment of Massalia, demand for tin seems to have increased. The Loire and Garonne became ever more important delivery and redistribution points; some of the foreign goods eventually reached Languedoc or the Alps via the Loire Valley. Several indigenous hillforts also seem to have adopted and imitated northern Italian vessels and jewellery. Finds from Cayla de Mailhac, for example, include northern Italian-style drinking wares and fibulae (Nash 2003, 245-246). Cart burials are also found at Gros-Guignon, Sénéret (Joffroy 1958), and throughout Poitou, Touraine, and Berry (Gallia 1961, 402; Gallia 1965, 375; Hodson and Rowlett 1973, 178; Willaume 1985).

The Mediterranean coast is also noted as having small boats transporting goods to and from the Tyrrhenian shore and Catalonia. Rothenberg and Bianco-Freijerio illustrate the possibility that tin ingots once thought to have been transported by sea from Tartessos, actually originated in the north Atlantic. During the seventh century, Italian ships also utilised the Mediterranean for transport (1981, 182).

2.3.3 Pottery and jewellery

It is possible to suggest separate routes used to transport slaves and other commodities: Switzerland and Germany may have been supplied by the Ticino-Mesocco-Bernadino-Rhine route (De Navarro 1928, 437-438). This route is supported by the distribution of several Etruscan items: cordoned buckets, the gold pendant from Canton of Berne (Déchelette Manual II, 2, p. 238f), and the spits found at Chalon-sur-Saône and Somme Bionne. Beaked flagons, possibly of Etruscan origin, have also been discovered throughout Switzerland. Other copies of Greek or Graeco-Italian wares may have had precursors in the transalpine region. However, it must be remembered that Etruscan transalpine trade was probably insubstantial prior to the occupation of Bologna after 500 BC. Therefore, it is possible that any Etruscan wares may have taken a sea-route to Massalia from central Italy. They would then have been distributed from southern France as has been suggested for the Etruscan flagons found at Vix, Hatten and Alsace (Megaw 1966, 39-40).

2.3.4 Slaves and other perishable goods

Unfortunately, many trade routes for items described by ancient literary sources, such as slaves, are unknown. As will be discussed below, no evidence survives in Massalia to substantiate the presence of any Celtic imports. All ideas concerning the distribution of Celtic slaves must therefore be based on literary evidence and the little archaeological evidence from other Mediterranean sites.

It is widely, but cautiously, assumed that human labour was used domestically on either side of the Alps. While no convincing documentary evidence demonstrating Celtic slaves present in Metropolitan Greece has been found, there is little reason to dismiss the idea altogether. Taylor (2001) demonstrates that some slaves in Greece were of Thracian and middle eastern origin; Homer (Od. I.136-43, 356-8, 397-8) describes the presence of foreign slaves. In western Etruria, late sixth century BC tomb paintings may depict slaves. In these paintings, the Greeks are shown with black hair, while other people are portrayed with qualities associated with northern Europeans (Nash 2003, 248-249). The tomb painting from Tomba del Giocolieri, Tarquinia demonstrates a red-haired, fair-skinned, amber-eyed girl (EP no. 70, c. 510 BC), for instance. Others show blonde haired musicians, jockeys, and people weaving garlands (EP no. 44, c. 510/500 BC; EP no.50, c. 510 BC respectively). While these characteristics may demonstrate European origin, there is nothing to indicate any direct source other than the generalised location.

Other items were most likely transported by sea or via river routes, possibly through southern France. This is the proposed method for the transport of more luxurious items. Examples include the "Rhodian" trefoil-mouth large handled bronze jugs found at Vilsingen (Germany) and Pertuis (Provence) (Shefton 1979, 22, 66, no. A18; Bouloumié 1978), the Italo-Greek hydria from Grächwil and Nîmes, and the Ste. Colombe tripod cauldron (Villard 1960, 132-133; Rolley 1962). No more precise route has been offered for the dispersal of these goods.

---

[3] Several hoards containing Gallic coins have been found in Britain (Allen 1961; 1971, 25-30; De Jersey 1999, 202). For discussion, chonology and lists of imported Massaliote and Gallic imitations of Massaliote and Macedonian coins see Allen 1960; Haselgrove 1978; 1987; Van Arsdell 1989, 2-7, 64-69, 428-429. The earliest coinage minted in Britain are also imitations of Massaliote bronze coinage (Van Ardsell 1989, 7-8). Similarly, a few examples of Greek goods have been found in Britain (Penhallurick 1986, 140-141).

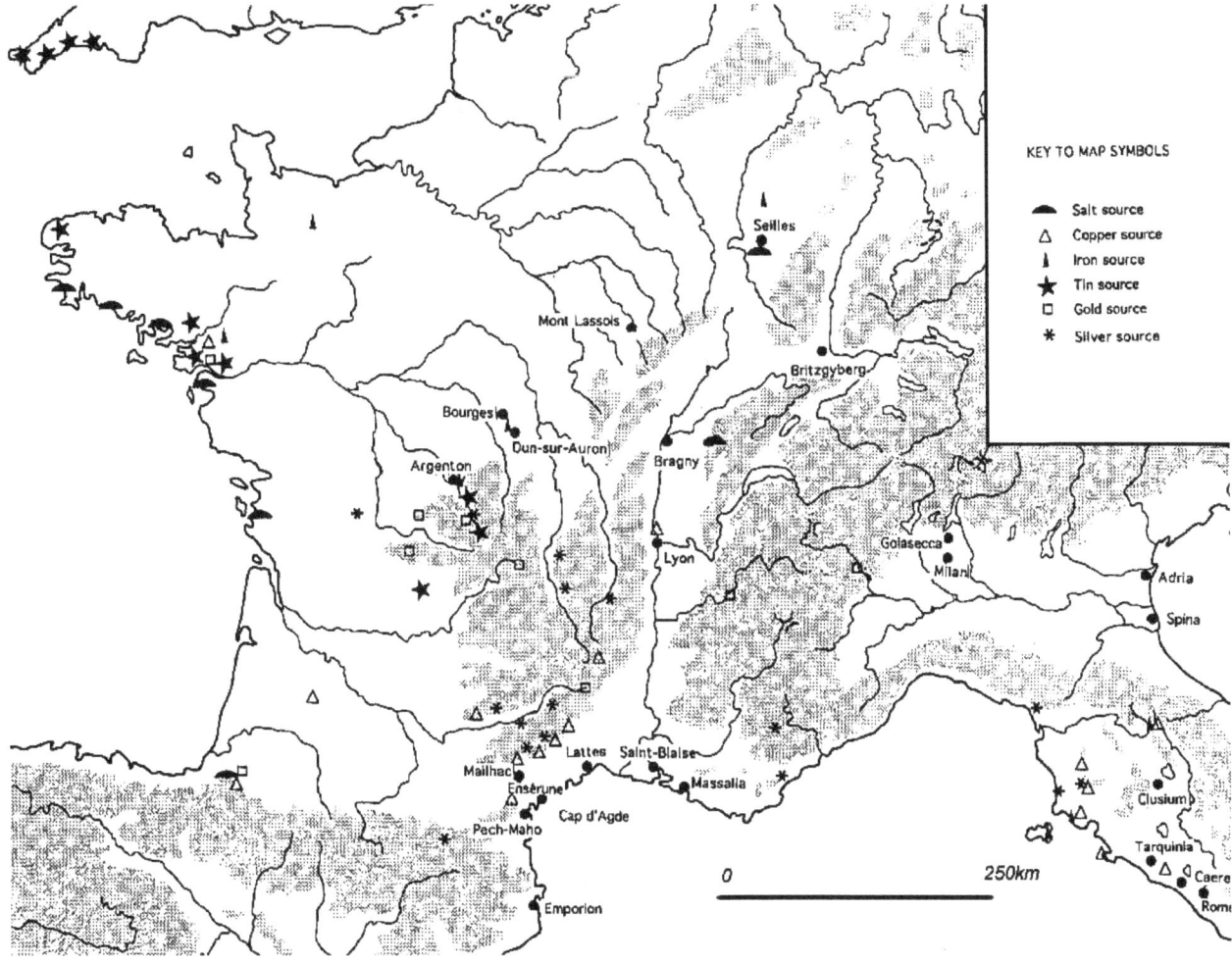

Figure 2.3: Distribution map of natural resources available in Gaul (Nash 2003, 245, fig. 1)

2.4 Reasons for Celtic-Greek trade: Celtic imports?

Aside from the continual problem of determining the provenance of imported objects, another problem remains: why did the Greeks engage in trade with the Celts?

Although Massalia had a large natural harbour, easily defended hills, islands which helped to safeguard its shores, and possibly a dominant position in the economic exchange of goods between the Mediterranean and the Gauls, it was not completely autonomous. Massalia had limited fertile land of its own. As a result, the Massaliotes may have needed to rely on the surrounding areas and hillforts for raw and natural materials. This may have been the initial incentive to establish trade relationships with northern and central Gaul. While it has been demonstrated above that the Celtic strongholds were importing luxury goods from Greece and Italy, Massalia was probably also importing Gallic products. However, no evidence has been found within the colony (discussed below).

Gaul was rich in natural resources (Figure 2.3). Sources of gold, copper, iron, tin and silver were particularly abundant in the western regions and the Massif Central, while naturally occurring sources of salt could be found on the Atlantic coast and in the eastern Massif Central. These materials were in demand by Gallic tribes, Greek colonies, and Mediterranean cities.

Conversely, Gaul was also a source of slaves. While it is not possible to reconstruct trade routes used to transport slaves, it may be possible to suggest the areas which were responsible for their supply. The Hunsrück-Eifel culture was probably the richest source. This warrior society was located in the middle Rhineland and Champagne. While the peaceful Hallstatt communities of western Gaul established diplomatic relations through trade, the Hunsrück-Eifel culture lived by raiding, the provision of slaves, and through hire as mercenaries (Nash 1985, 48-52).

The difficulty in understanding the Greek trade impetus lies in the fact that there is little to no archaeological evidence within Greek cities for trade with central Europe (Wells 1984, 108). Thus, all theories must be based on the Mediterranean goods that can be found in Celtic strongholds. However, as demonstrated above, the goods most likely needed by Massalia are raw materials. Many of these materials would either have been incorporated into locally-produced goods, such as pottery or metal objects, or have been consumed. The goods that would not have been used in industrial production are items that would not be readily preserved in the archaeological record. For example, textiles are found only in the rarest of conditions. Likewise, slaves and the lower classes of society leave little behind with which to detect their presence. Additionally, the method of transport may not be one which is readily preserved. Goods were often shipped in barrels which are not usually preserved in the archaeological record except under special environmental circumstances. Therefore, the bias of the archaeological record may explain the lack of evidence for Gallic exports: perishable and naturally occurring items would have deteriorated, as would the cases in which they were shipped.

CHAPTER 3
GALLO-GREEK RELATIONS, SEVENTH CENTURY – FIFTH CENTURY BC

3.1 West central Europe, the Hallstatt Zone

By the late Hallstatt period, numerous hillforts throughout eastern France, Switzerland, and southern Germany had been established. Most are now thought to have been fürstensitze (Kimmig 1968), the residences of chieftains or tribal leaders. Although associated with contemporary settlements, most of these sites are known only through the archaeological remains of the various élite burials (fürstengräber) situated in proximity to the hillforts to which they presumably belonged.

Around the same time, Massalia was founded by the Greeks, who quickly established long-distance trade routes, engaging in direct commerce with the Celtic leaders (Sanders 1957, 349-350). Mediterranean goods found within the Celtic tumuli demonstrate demand and supply between the Greek colony and the Celtic strongholds. Imported luxury goods are not only confined to these élite sites, but have also been discovered in burials throughout Gaul: Somme Bonne (Marne Valley), La Motte St. Valentine (Haute Marne), and Rodenbach (Rhenish Palatinate). However, particular attention has been paid to the tumuli at the Heuneberg in the upper Danube (Kimmig 1968; Kimmig and Gersbach 1971), Höhenasperg (Zürn 1970), and Mont Lassois in Burgundy (Joffroy 1960). These sites have yielded some of the most unique Greek imported luxury items found within central and northern Gaul.

3.1.1 The Heuneberg

The Heuneberg is located on a terrace above a ford of the Danube. It is one of the smallest sites of its kind. Extensive excavation of the settlement area has demonstrated that the site was in use as early as the fifteenth to thirteenth centuries BC. As it was not continuously occupied, habitation layers were separated by phases of inactivity. In one particular instance, dated to the sixth century BC, a period of abandonment was followed by a phase of intense building activity: a dozen walls were erected around a citadel and a series of settlements were constructed inside the defended area. The latest wall discovered was destroyed by fire in the fifth century BC, after which the area was inactive until the middle ages (Kimmig 1975, 36-38).

During this brief phase of occupation, a number of interesting changes take place. Many of these circulate around the replacement of Celtic construction techniques by Mediterranean ones. The fortifications of the Heuneberg were originally constructed of local wood, earth, and stone. During the first half of the sixth century, these defensive circuits were reconstructed. The new walls had limestone foundations and were composed of mud-brick. Several square bastions were also built (Dehn 1958, 55-62). In addition to these changes, excavation of one-third of the inner fortress has demonstrated the division of land into "quarters." Each quarter had a particular function. While some were associated with houses, others were used for industry and production. For instance, smelting furnaces and smoke outlets contained thousands of small bronze pellets, indicating metal working (Kimmig 1975, 51). In the south-east corner of the citadel, conversely, individual farmsteads had associated storage pits and were separated from each other by fences.

Similar changes are demonstrated by the ceramic assemblages found within the settlement. Several types of imported Mediterranean pottery were discovered: attic black-figure cups, kraters (used in ancient Greek culture to mix wine and water), wares attributed to the Este culture, fragments of amphorae (many of which are Massaliote types), and jugs dating between 540 and 480 BC (Wells 1984, 111; Biel 2006, 4-5). Although locally-produced items were also present, many of these were manufactured using Mediterranean techniques and equipment such as the fast wheel. Similarly, extremely high-quality painted pottery was produced as were local imitations of Mediterranean jugs, indicated by the casting model of an attachment shaped like an Etruscan silen (Biel 2006, 4-5). The presence of amber from the Baltic region (Kimming 1975, 56) also suggests that goods were not solely imported from Mediterranean regions, but from a wider geographic area. Despite the numerous imports, there is evidence attesting to the local-production of several new indigenous forms, different from those found in the surrounding burial mounds (see below).

The Heuneberg is surrounded by numerous tumuli, many of which are contemporary with the Hallstatt occupation (Figure 3.1). These burials are situated on top of an extramural settlement which, so far, has proven to be unique.[1] The oldest of the associated burial mounds is Hohmichele Grave VI; it stands 13m high and 100m wide. The central funerary chamber, which held a double burial of a man and a woman, was completely robbed. However,

---
[1] No other examples of external settlements have been discovered at any of the other *fürstensitze* in the area, including Hochdorf and Hohenasperg (Biel 2006, 4).

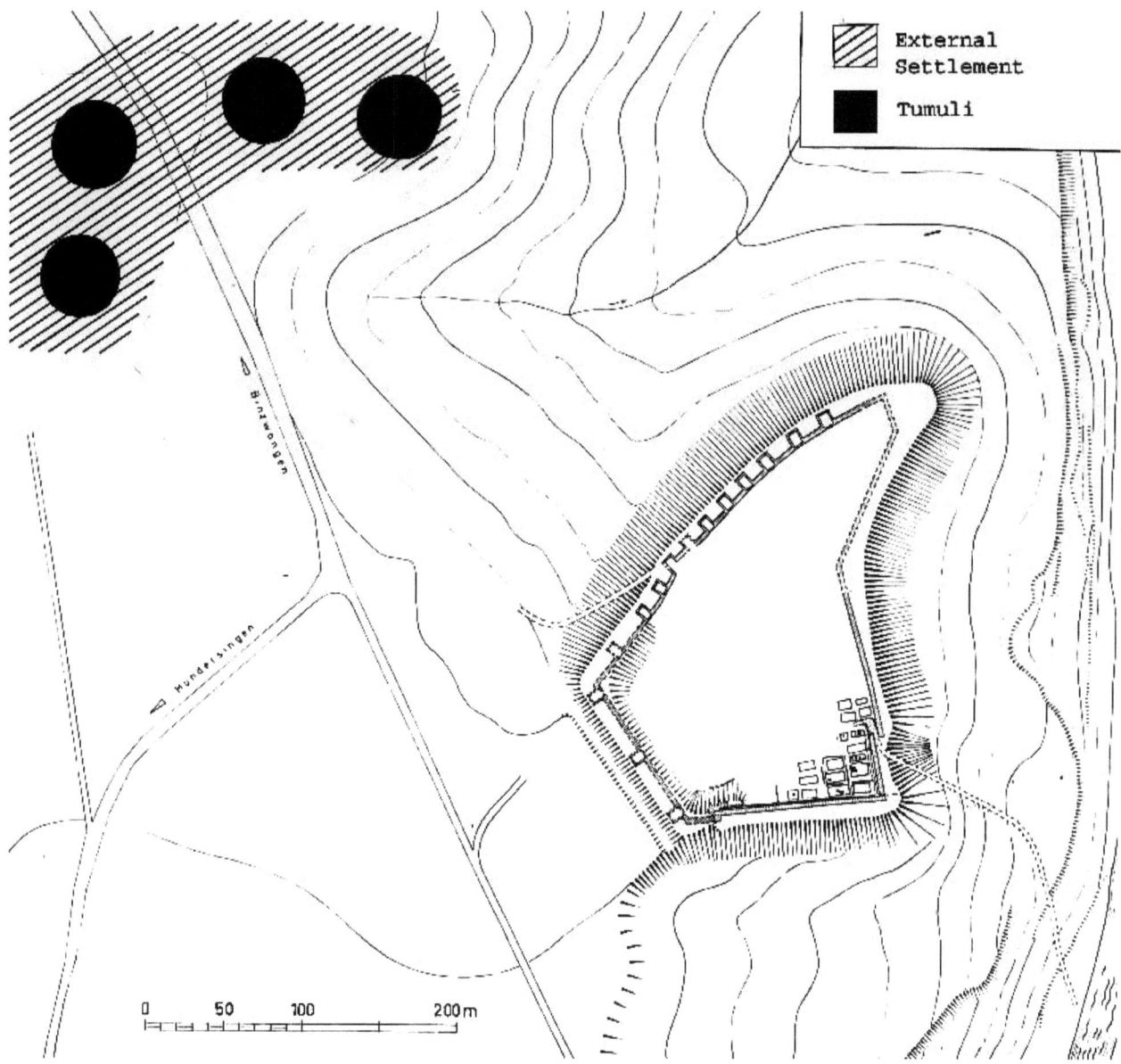

Figure 3.1: Site plan of the Heuneberg, external settlement and its overlying tumuli (After Kimmig 1991, 114)

several artefacts were recovered from a side compartment. Among them were a four-wheel wagon, bronze vessels, and various smaller objects. Of the other mounds excavated, none yielded finds which were indicative of foreign influence or trade. On the contrary, the items were fairly characteristic of the late Hallstatt (ie harnasses, gold necklaces and bronze vessels) and were of Celtic manufacture and origin (Biel 2006, 4).

3.1.2 Höhenapsberg

What little is known about the settlements at Höhenasperg has been provided through rescue excavations; the site had been badly damaged during the medieval and modern periods. Consequently, reconstructions are primarily based on the surrounding burials (Biel 1981, 16). The settlements seem to have consisted of unfortified hamlets of limited size, the locations of which appear to have shifted during the late Hallstatt period and the early phases of the La Tène (Biel 2006, 7).

Höhenasperg is surrounded by rich burials in the form of tumuli (Figure 3.2). The closest are Grafenbühl, Klein Aspergle (Jacobsthal 1944; Kimmig 1988), and two others which have yet to be excavated. Situated still further from Höhenasperg are Römerhügel at Ludwigsburg (Paret 1935, 19f.), two graves at Stuttgart-Bad Cannstatt (Paret 1935; 1938b, 60ff.), Esslingen-Sirnau (Paret 1938a, 55ff.), and to the west the tomb of Schöckingen (Paret 1952, 37ff.). Various others are still awaiting excavation. It must be noted that while there are many tumuli situated at a distance from the fürstensitze of Hochdorf, their relationship to the tribal site is unknown (Frankenstein and Rowlands 1978). The three oldest burials, Hochdorf, Grafenbühl, and Klein Aspergle, are the key sites.

HOCHDORF

As mentioned above, very little is known about the settlements which are associated with the rich burials in the surrounding countryside. However, the discovery

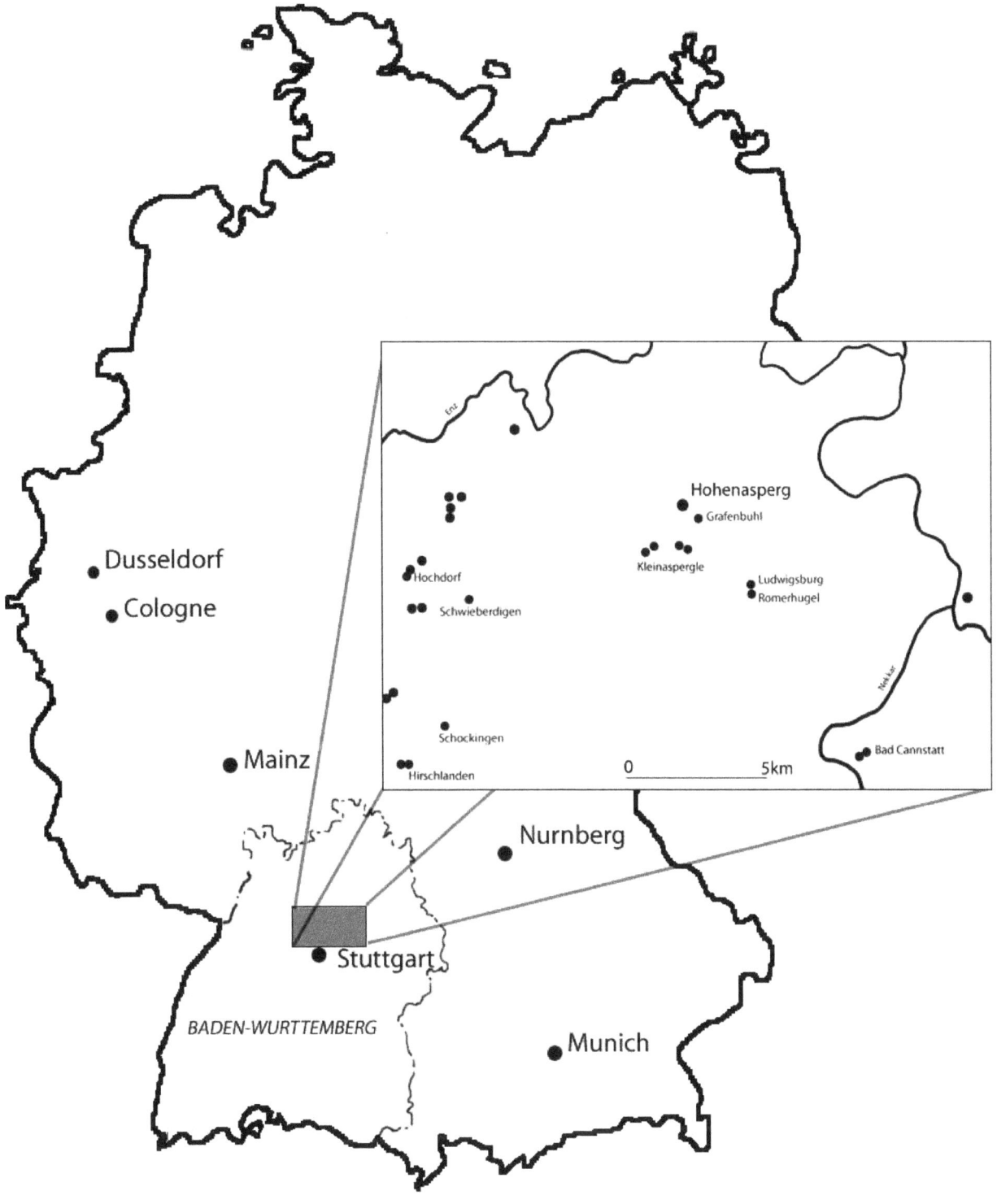

Figure 3.2: Map of tumuli in the area surrounding Hohenasperg

of Hochdorf led to the systematic excavation of a 3ha area located just above the iron age settlement. Various structures were found including large houses 140 sqm in size, sunken floor huts measuring between 3 and 8m long, storage pits, and possibly granaries. Structures were arranged in a rectangular system, indicating a planned settlement. Wheel-turned local pottery and six red-figure Attic shards from kylikes have provided a rough date for the settlement around 425 BC. Other artefacts - a balance with a scale to tare and cast bronze imports – were also recovered (Biel 2006, 7-8).

The Hochdorf tumulus dates to c. 550 BC. Although badly damaged, the tumulus has an unusual stone construction. The monumental façades have an entrance which is formed by two stone walls between which is a paved earthen ramp (Biel 2006, 5-6). The wooden central burial chamber was enclosed in a larger wooden chamber and the space in between filled with large stones. The caution taken in securing the burial indicates a concern with the tomb being robbed after it was sealed. These constructions have not previously been attested in the western Hallstatt region, but are more akin to eastern Hallstatt funerary traditions found in eastern Austria and northern Yugoslavia (Biel 1981, 16-17). This may demonstrate the western flow of ideas stimulating a cultural response.

Before the discovery of Hochdorf, most grave goods were recovered from the undisturbed side chambers of tombs. These artefacts were generally less lavish than those which would have been placed directly in the main burial chamber with the body of the deceased. Due to the extra care taken when constructing the Hochdorf burial mound, the central chamber was undisturbed and provided some of the richest finds from the Hallstatt period.

The skeleton was oriented north-south, with the head to the south – usual for the period – and was buried with a birch bark hat, antenna dagger, and torc. All these items attest to the high rank of the individual; they are similar to those portrayed by the life size stone statue of a Hallstatt prince (Figure 3.3) found 10km away at Hirschlanden (see Figure 3.2). Furthermore, the body was buried lying on a couch 3m long. The couch was decorated with "punch-line" technique and depicted a four-wheel wagon and three groups of dancers with swords (Figure 3.4). The feet were made of eight cast-bronze female figures (see Biel 1985, 110, pl. 30) which carried the seat on their hands. The women were each mounted on a wheel possibly to facilitate the lateral movement of the couch as opposed to being carried. Each figure was strengthened, supported, and held to one another by an elaborate iron frame.

No direct parallel, either artistically or technically, to this couch is known. The punch-line decoration, however, is similar to situla art, possibly indicating Etruscan influence from northern Italy and Istria (Biel 1981, 17). Regardless, there are two theories on the origin of manufacture: the local production by migrant Italian craftsmen or the importation from the Adriatic coast (Biel 2006, 6). Despite these various theories, no conclusive evidence exists to dismiss the idea of southern German manufacture. The representation of a couch with surrounding dancers, and the technique used to produce the decoration may indeed allude to influence from upper Greek or Italian rituals. Nevertheless, it cannot be viewed as proof that it was manufactured in Greece or Italy.

Although Mediterranean influence is attested by the presence of many of the finds, the Hochdorf grave goods also demonstrate the preservation of indigenous rites and ideals. Drinking horns were found, as were many personal items such as combs, razors, torcs, a belt, iron dagger with a gold sheath, and a broad armlet. The richness of the grave is further indicated by the unusual finds of gold serpentine fibulae and a pair of gold-adorned leather shoes with pointed toes. These were decorated with the same punch work as the couch, suggesting a similar origin or manufacture in the same workshop (Biel 1981, 17). Furthermore, clothing and fabric were preserved by the copper oxides from the bronze metal work of the couch.

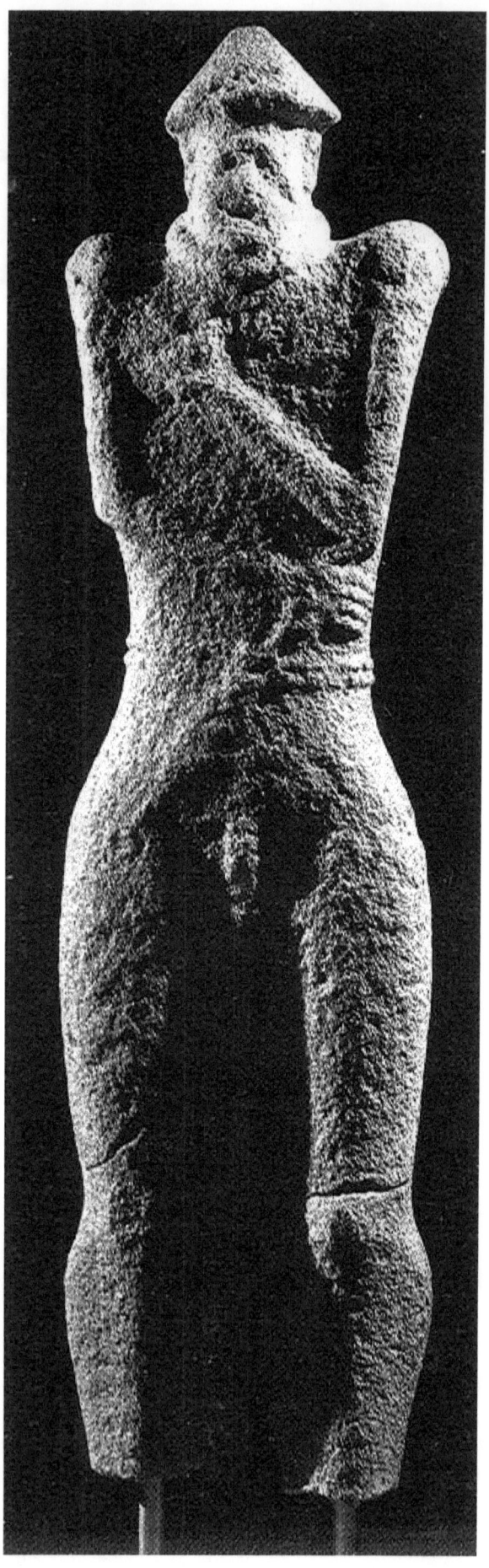

Figure 3.3: Statue of Hallstatt prince found near Hirschlanden (Frey 1991a, 88)

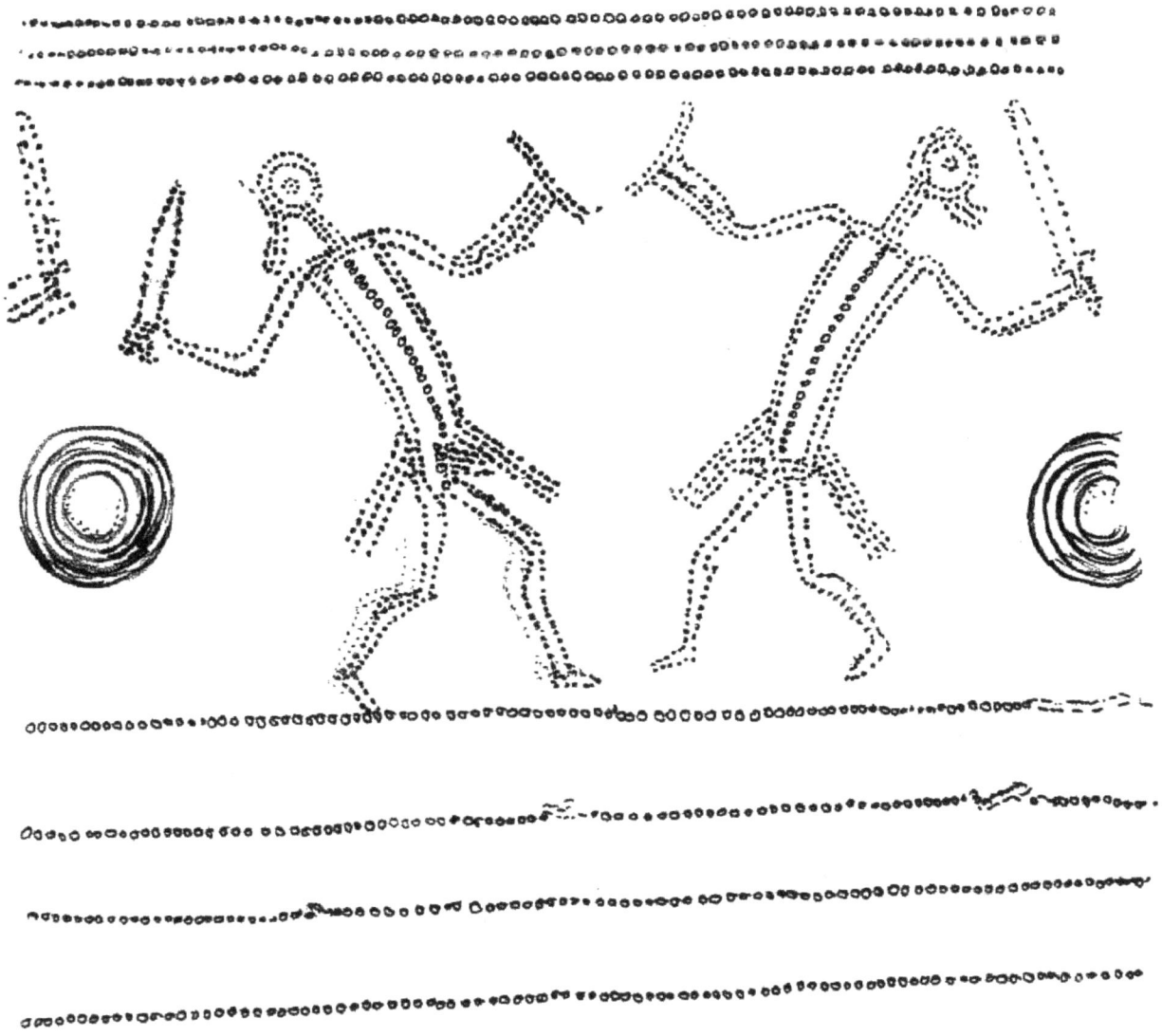

Figure 3.4: Punch decoration on burial couch from Hochdorf. The couch, although of questionable provenance, alludes to Mediterranean influence both in ornamentation technique and theme: the punch-line decoration employed a technique similar to that of situla art, originating in Northern Italy and Istria, while the dancing figures illustrate Mediterranean funerary festivities (Drawing L. Laing)

In addition to locally produced items, and those goods of more questionable origin, ie the couch, were goods clearly imported from the south. One item that has gained much attention is the bronze cauldron. It has a round base with an inwardly curving rim, and is decorated with three large, crouching, cast bronze lions alternating with bronze handles. It has been widely accepted that this is the product of classical workmanship, probably originating from a Greek colony in lower Italy. However, it is interesting to note that one of the three lions is both compositionally different and of inferior quality: the body lacks the naturalism the other two lions possess (although one had a casting defect fixed by the application of lead). The difference in style might be attributable to a local bronze caster, who did not have knowledge of the anatomy of a lion and the skill of the original craftsman. The second lion (see Biel 1985, 122, pl.34), although the quality indicates classical craftsmanship, is engraved. The mane is depicted by stacked lyre scroll engraving (see Biel 1985, 119, fig. 69), a design usually identified with the early La Tène period. Biel (1981, 29) has noted that both the lions and the handles were attached to the cauldron by rough hammering, indicating that both were not part of the vessel's initial manufacture, but were later additions. Equally, this could suggest that the cauldron was damaged and subsequently repaired locally.

Residue analysis has shown that this vessel contained pollen, and more specifically, locally made mead (Biel 1981, 17; Biel 2006 6). Usually Greek kraters, such as this one from Hochdorf, would be accompanied by a Greek tripod. In this instance, the tripod was substituted by a wooden structure covered with badger skins (Biel 1981, 17).

GRAFENBÜHL

Grafenbühl is younger than Hochdorf; it was constructed around 500 BC. The central chamber was looted, and the few artefacts recovered were found in a side chamber.

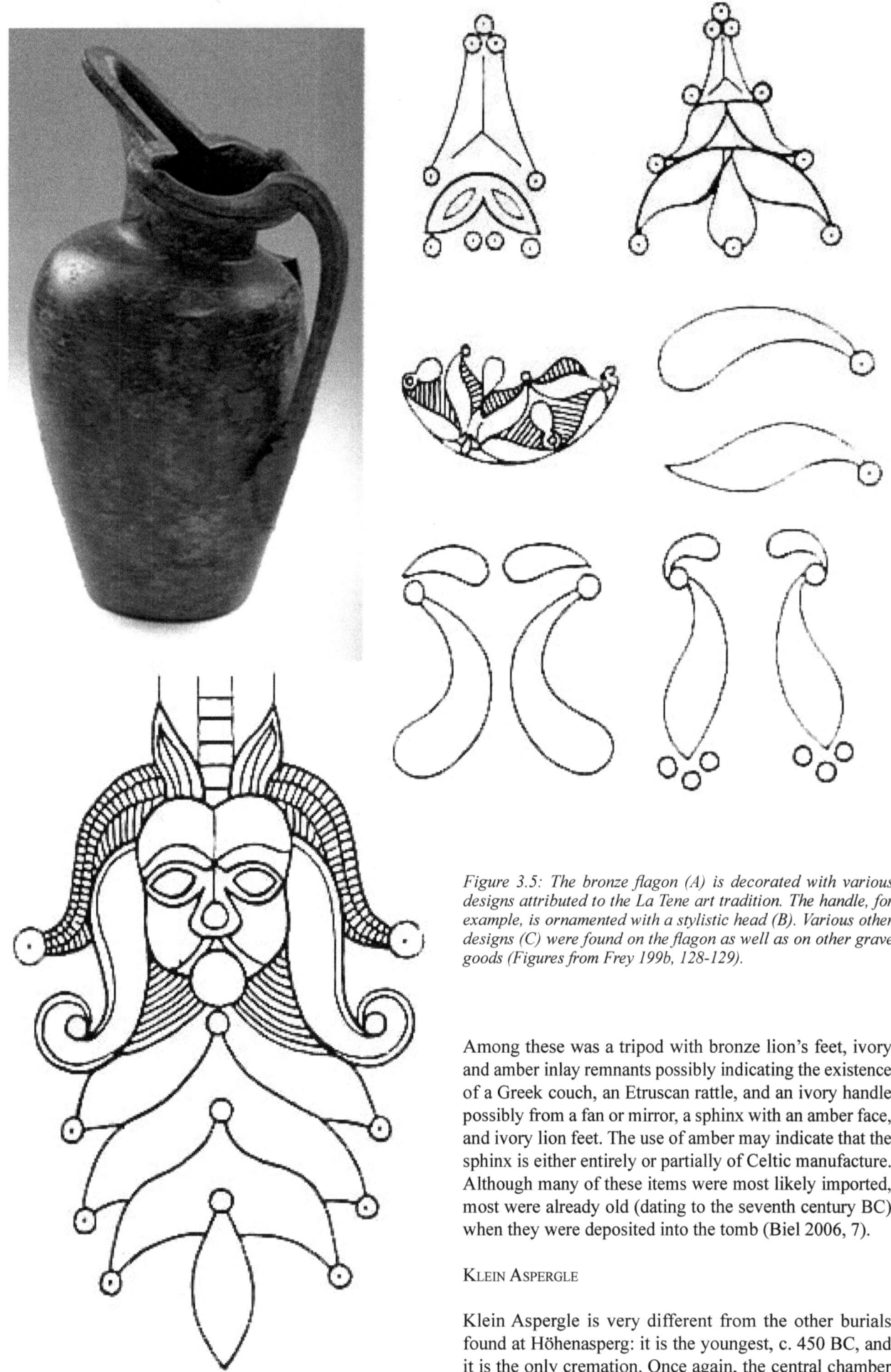

Figure 3.5: The bronze flagon (A) is decorated with various designs attributed to the La Tene art tradition. The handle, for example, is ornamented with a stylistic head (B). Various other designs (C) were found on the flagon as well as on other grave goods (Figures from Frey 199b, 128-129).

Among these was a tripod with bronze lion's feet, ivory and amber inlay remnants possibly indicating the existence of a Greek couch, an Etruscan rattle, and an ivory handle possibly from a fan or mirror, a sphinx with an amber face, and ivory lion feet. The use of amber may indicate that the sphinx is either entirely or partially of Celtic manufacture. Although many of these items were most likely imported, most were already old (dating to the seventh century BC) when they were deposited into the tomb (Biel 2006, 7).

KLEIN ASPERGLE

Klein Aspergle is very different from the other burials found at Höhenasperg: it is the youngest, c. 450 BC, and it is the only cremation. Once again, the central chamber had been robbed and the artefacts recovered from a lateral chamber. Several of the items were imported: a cauldron, Etruscan bronze stamnos, Italic ribbed bucket, and two Attic red-figure cups dating to the mid-fifth century BC. Other items demonstrate styles typical of the early La Tène period and attest to the preservation of indigenous festivities. Among these artefacts were the ends of two drinking horns, clothing, and gold necklaces. One item is of particular importance and interest - a beaked flagon, or schnabelkanne.

The beaked flagon (Figure 3.5a) was a locally-produced imitation of an Etruscan model. This is evidenced in the different proportions of the body: the shoulders project horizontally, the base is longer and slightly curved, and it is decorated with La Tène art. At the bottom of the handle is a Celtic depiction of a head (Figure 3.5b). The pointed ears, similar to those found on the joints of the Etruscan stamnos also from this tomb, protrude above the head. The eyes, cheeks, nose, chin and forehead are all depicted spherically while the beard is represented by overlapping palmette leaves and has no distinct edges. Similar figures appear on the upper part of the handle. Other less pronounced representations of animals can be found on the lateral extensions of the handle (Figure 3.5c) (Frey 1991b, 127-128). This singular find has lead to the conclusion that Klein Aspergle was the first and only La Tène burial within the Höhenasperg Hallstatt tumuli.

3.1.3 The Vix burial, Mont Lassois

The Vix burial is located near Châtillon-sur-Seine, just below the Celtic hillfort of Mont Lassois. A lot of indigenous material typical of the late Hallstatt was uncovered within the stronghold. This resulted in Mont Lassois becoming a key site in the establishment of an extended chronology for the final phase of the Hallstatt culture, and further defining the first stages of the second iron age (Dehn and Frey, 1962).

Much like Hochdorf, the central chamber of the burial remained intact and undisturbed until its discovery in 1953. While the grave goods do not allow for a precise date for the burial itself, a terminus post quem of c. 500 BC was established by the Attic black-figure "Droop" cup[2] (Megaw 1966, 38). The famous Vix krater also cannot be dated. It is older than most of the other finds in the burial, most likely dating to the end of the first quarter of the sixth century BC. This date is usually based on the stylistic comparison to Attic black-figure pottery transported on the proposed Massalia-Burgundy-Jura-Danube trade route (Megaw 1966, 41) - an idea that is problematic. These Attic black-figure ceramics mainly date to the mid-sixth century and can only demonstrate (if anything) the comparatively short amount of time that this particular type of Attic wares was in high demand (Dehn and Frey 1962, 200). Consequently, the krater may allow (at best) for a restricted chronology of the mid-sixth century to be determined.

The Vix krater (Figure 3.6a) is a very interesting find: it is the largest bronze vessel of the Greek Archaic Period in existence (Megaw 1966, 38). The sheer size (1.63m) and weight (208.6kg) would have made transport a problem. It is possible that it was dismantled after manufacture and reassembled upon arrival at its destination. The discovery of an alpha-numeric key, possibly utilized to fix the position of the figure decorations, may support of this idea. There are several places in which decoration defacement occurs. This presumably took place after the initial assembly, when it was dismantled to be transported north (Amandry 1954, 125-140). The rarity of the krater, combined with the efforts that must have been taken to transport it over long distances, is demonstrative of its importance and its prestige.

The origin of the krater has also proven to be problematic. Many scholars have again relied on artistic comparisons to enable some form of provenance to be established. There are several stylistic parallels to goods produced in mainland Greece during the middle Corinthian III (AJA, LXII 1958, 198 and n. 13). During this time, repeating friezes of separately attached auriga-hoplite-quadriga figures were popular, as is exemplified by the Chest of Cypselus[3] (Figure 3.6b). While some scholars suggest an origin in mainland Greece because of this, others propose that the script of the alpha-numeric code may denote an origin in a Laconian or Tarentine workshop (Megaw 1966, 39). It is important to note, however, that while the language of the script may suggest movement, it does not necessarily indicate provenance.

Another important find is the gold "diadem," now thought to be a torc. Its origin is still a matter of debate. Although the design of the filigree on the terminal pads (see Berthelier-Ajot 1991, 117) is of Greek quality and character, there is no reason to believe that any of it originated in Greek or Etruscan workshops (Eluère 1987a; Joffroy 1954, 46-8; Kimmig 1958, 85). If the scale is changed, parallels can be drawn to eastern jewellery traditions. The horses are similar to those found in art of the Steppes (Rosen-Przeworska 1964a; 1964b, 131) and the renderings of the shoulder-spirals and stabbed pelt recall Scythian traditions (Harding 2007, 63; Maxwell-Hyslop 1971, 196f., pl. 149-152). Manufacture could therefore be of Graeco-Scythian origin and attributed to a Greek craftsman located on the north shore of the Black Sea (Joffroy 1960, 105-106). Likewise, there can be no dismissal of indigenous influence from the Hallstatt Goldreifen (Hawkes 1963, 10-11; Uenze 1964, 110). Regardless, it is now thought that the Vix torc was produced by Celts approximately around 500 BC[4] (Eluère 1990, 21, pl. 13; Eluère et al 1989).

---

[2] The "Droop" cup has been determined to have been decorated between 530 and 520 BC. Its stylistic affinities have been attributed to the "Wraith" painter. For a full discussion see Beazley 1956, 201 and no. 14.

[3] The Chest of Cypselus was a chest adorned with gold, ivory, and cedar wood figures depicting various scenes of Greek myth. It was a devotional offering at Olympia and described by Pausanias (5.16.5- 5.19.10) in the second century AD. Unfortunately, the chest has since been lost and reconstructions rely heavily on literary sources. For discussions of the chest and/or its graphic representation see Burgess 2004, 86-89; Jones 1894; Murray 2004, 47, 61-64; Snodgrass 1998, 110-116, 2001.

[4] For detailed analysis of composition and manufacturing techniques see Eluère 1991, 352; Guerra and Calligaro 2003, 1530; Nicolini 1995, 461-463. For descriptions of gold-working practices in the pre-Roman Iron Age, see Eluère 1987b.

Culture Contact in Southern Mediterranean France

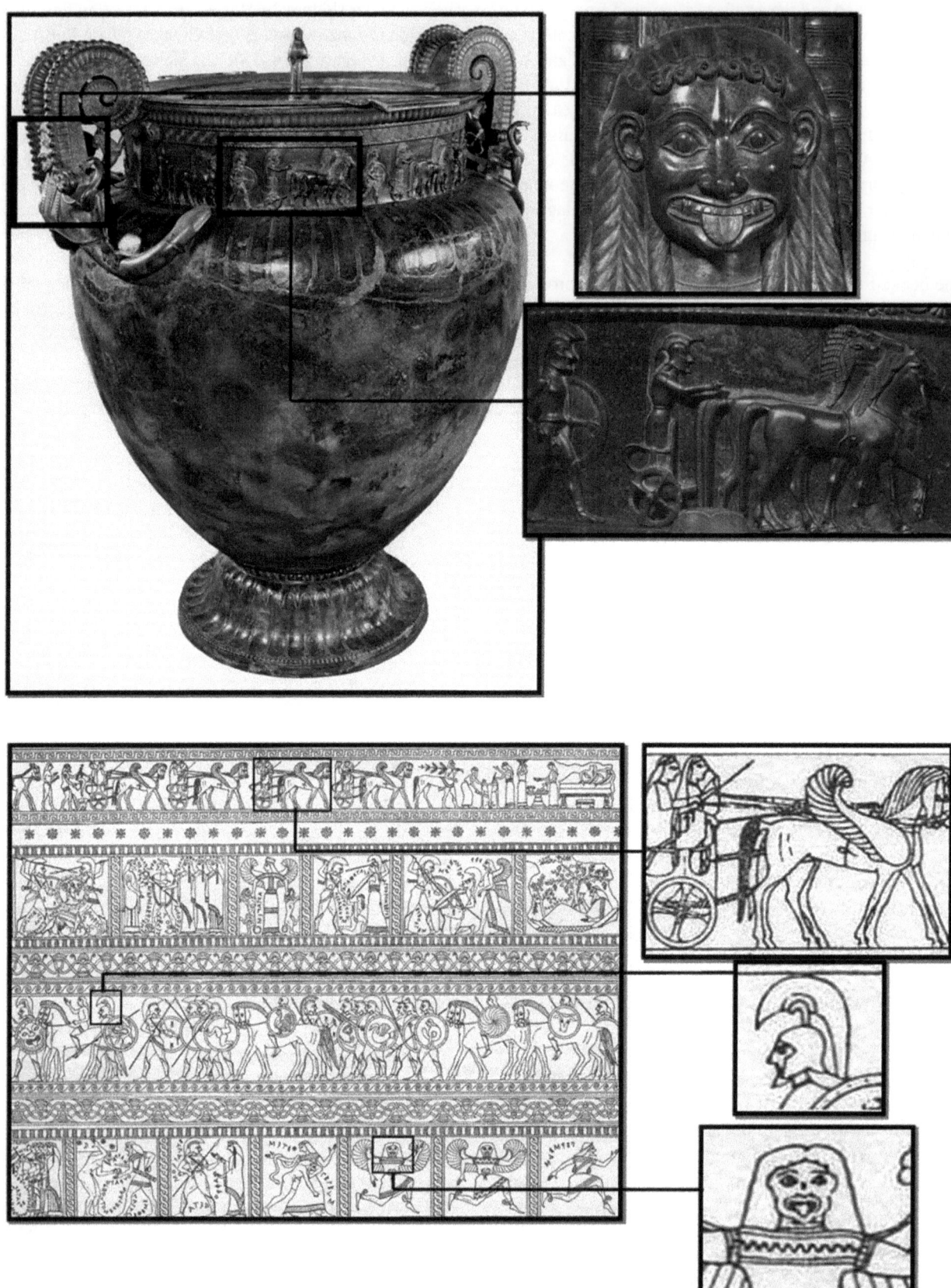

Figure 3.6: The Chest of Cypselus (B) was made in Corinth during the 6th century BC. Because of the similarities in the decorations and the figures, it has been suggested that the Vix Krater (A) may have the same provenance (A: After Joffroy 1957, pls. 1, 6, 9l B: After Massow 1916, 1ff., pl. 10)

3.2 Celtic strongholds and Greek ports

It is often debated whether or not the relatively contemporaneous sixth-century foundation of the Greek port of Massalia and the rise of powerful Celtic kingdoms several kilometres to the north was coincidental (Villard 1960, 76-81; Morel 1975, 866f). Some scholars argue that it was more than just chance. If social position in Celtic society was dependent on the control of commerce to and from the outside world, then political power would have been derived by the conduct of trade with the Greek colony. Individual political power in Celtic society may have been strengthened by the ability to engage in trade. However, the establishment of autonomous chiefdoms should not be thought to have been built upon commercial contact. Aside from the items being traded, travelling in the early iron age was most likely an arduous and long undertaking. As a result, the transport of foreign items would probably be more justified if an established trade or influential centre of power was the destination. Regions lacking these structures, likewise, would be less likely to be in contact or in a position to exchange goods (Biel 2006, 5). It must also be remembered that no merchandise exchanges can be known with any degree of certainty; therefore, the discovery of Greek imports in an area is simply an indicator of trade.

The distribution of Mediterranean goods in northern and central Gaul is geographically restricted: many Greek and Etruscan objects dating to the seventh-fifth centuries geographically occur on trade routes along which Mont Lassois, Höhenasperg and the Heuneburg are situated. It must be said that imports are not only found in this region. Several sites in southern Gaul, particularly those located in the lower Rhône Basin, have yielded evidence of Mediterranean contact.[5] However, the character and nature of these goods is dramatically different to those found in the north and central regions. In general, the assemblages consist of simple wine amphorae and smaller vessels associated with wine consumption. The goods are, therefore, less spectacular in scale, and are rarely found in association with burials (Dietler 1995, 67). The difference is usually attributed to different settlement patterns and the associated social differences.[6] Outside west central Europe, society was not necessarily hierarchical or centralised. Central and northern Gaul not only have fürstensitze, but also demonstrate the existence of other detached settlements. Most of these lesser sites were separated by at least 100km. Conversely, further east were early iron age hillforts at Stična, Sopron, and Burgberg near Großmugl. These were older than those strongholds associated with the chieftain burials, but have not yielded any finds of Greek imports. In Bavaria, the higher classes lived in herensitze, defended farmsteads (Biel 2006, 5). Similarly, social ideals would have differed among these regions (Nash 1985, 48-52).

At the end of the fifth century, Hallstatt D transitioned into La Tène I, signalling both a cultural change and a geographic shift in Celtic strongholds. The rich sites associated with the fürstengräber, such as Mont Lassois and the Heuneberg, were abandoned. Conversely, the Marne Valley in France and the Hunsrück-Eifel region in the middle Rhineland began to demonstrate patterns of urban development (Biel 2006, 9). These new areas of political power increasingly engaged in Mediterranean trade with the Graeco-Etruscan ports of Adria and Spina, located on the Po delta (Kimmig 1975, 44-46). It was thought that, because of these changes, North and central Gaul were left without centres of importation and distribution, and moreover, without links to Massalia. The Greek port, likewise, was supposedly forced to confine trade to local markets, not only strengthening Mediterranean influence along the coast and southern Gaul, but allowing the La Tène culture to develop without Hellenic contact for two centuries. Consequently, it has been suggested that the spread of the La Tène culture contributed, if not caused, Massaliote trade with central and northern Gaul to decline and the systematic end of princely sites (King 1990, 16-17).

The decline of princely sites is perhaps better attributed to the break-up of society and/or the adoption or adaptation of Hellenic ideals. As time progressed, Mediterranean imports became more frequent, as did the degradation of quality. Smaller and less expensive objects began to be imported more often, and eventually Attic ceramics and indigenous copies became prominent (see chapter 4). Southern ideas were adapted to fit Celtic styles. Southern habits, as is demonstrated by the chariot burials associated with dining in the prone position, were imitated by the indigenous population (Biel 2006, 7-8). Ultimately, this southern and Hellenic influence contributed, if not created, the distinctive La Tène artistic style (see pages 61-63).

While it is undeniable that the fifth century abandonment

---

[5] Artefacts dating to similar periods have been found on many southern Gallic sites. Some of these artefacts, like those in northern and central Gaul pre-date (seventh to sixth centuries BC) any Phocaean colonial establishment (Nickels et al 1981, 99; Villard 1960, 74 no. 5; Jully 1983, ii/1 1016, nos. 001-002). Examples include: three Corinthian-type cups from the Iron Age cemetery at Agde (Nickels et al 1981; Nickels 1989, 288-289; Bérard, Nickels and Schwaller 1990, 183-184), a Corinthian type cup from the Grand Basin I cemetery at Cayla de Mailhac (Louis et al 1958, 62-64 and fig. 48; Villard 1960, 74 and n.5; Nickels et al 1981, 100; Jully 1980, 480f and pl. A1), Eastern Greek bird bowls, a rosette skyphos and PC skyphos from Saint-Blaise (Rolland 1951, 59-63 and figs. 91-8; 1956, 51; 1964, 569-572; 1963, 81-89), a Corinthian olpe, Ionic cup, and Eastern Greek bird bowl at La Courronne (Lagrand 1959, 179-201). See Jully 1983, 349-350 for more examples. The Phocaeans of Massalia were not the only importers of foreign goods: for a discussion of pre-colonial contact, see Graham 2001; Morel 1995, 42-45. For Etruscan imports to southern Gaul see Rasmussen 2006, 104-106, pls. 31-32; Bouloumié 1979; Lagrand 1959; Py and Py 1974, 86, 141-254; Bouloumié 1976; Py 1985, 84; Long, Pomey and Sourisseau 2002; Landes et al 2003. It must be noted that most of these sites represent circumstances that are not wide-spread in southern Gaul at this time: Agde was a Massaliote comptoir, Saint-Blaise presents an interesting dichotomy of indigenous and Hellenic culture (discussed in Chapter 4) and has been hypothesized to have been under Massaliote control (Bouloumié and Borely 1992; Rolland 1951 nos. 3 and 7, 1956). La Courronne become a quarry supplying stone to Massalia and Saint-Blaise among others (for further discussion, see below). Barruol (1969, 224) suggested that it may also have been a Massaliote colony. Furthermore, it should be noted that little evidence dating before 600BC has been found at Marseille, and no true occupation has been recognized (Villard 1960, 76).

[6] See individual tribes of southern Gaul: Barruol 1969, 109-111; Taffanel and Taffanel 1960, 1-37; Bouloumié 1978, 219-240. See articles by Arnold, Fischer, and Dietler in Arnold and Gibson 1995, 34-72, for discussions of social structure and relations in areas with *fürstensitze* and *fürstengräber* (princely burials).

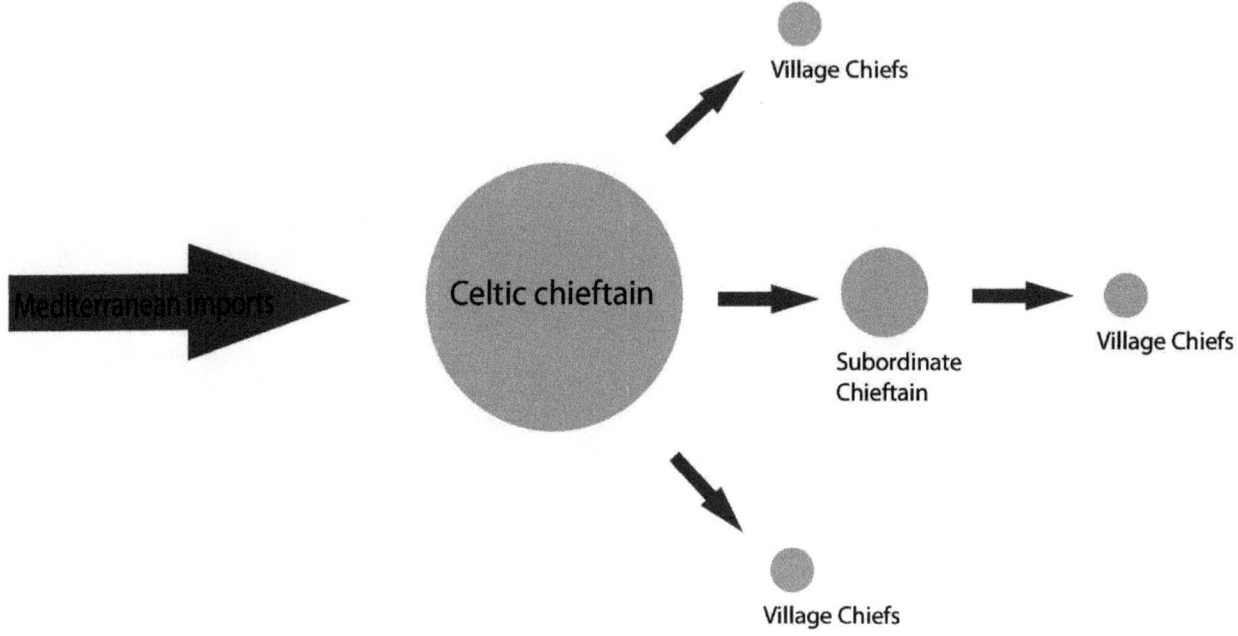

Figure 3.7: Diagram of proposed Hallstatt political structure (After Wells 1980, fig. 4.3)

of the princely sites did impact on the spread of Massaliote influence, the resultant loss of northern and central trade cannot be attributed solely to that reason. By the time the sites were abandoned, Greece had already lost its dominance of the seaways: the Carthaginians had closed sea-routes through the Straights of Gibraltar (Powell 1958, 94-98; Boardman 1964, 216-218). Furthermore, Greek, and specifically Massaliote, trade was not fully dependant on northern and central Gaul to sustain their role as a port or trade station, nor was it now completely dependant on local markets. Greek commerce was subsequently stimulated in the Adriatic Sea, and Iberia. Other areas included the southern Balkans, where Greek trade had initially been established during the in the seventh and sixth centuries (Alexander 1962, 123-130). Massalia had also become involved in the tin route, which brought tin from Britain and Amorica (see above). However, after the Persian-Phocaean battle of Alalia around 540 BC, the Phocaean colonies were left to fend for themselves and no longer had a direct source for Phocaean and other Greek wares. This is best demonstrated at Massalia by the termination of imported Greek pottery and its replacement by local material (Villard 1960; for a discussion see chapter 4). It has been suggested by Megaw (1966, 41) that because of this, the presence of sixth century Greek imports at Celtic hillforts demonstrates their importance as trade areas during a time when Persia and Phocaia were at war. This is highly unlikely.

The quality of the individual artefacts discovered at Mont Lassois, Höhenasperg and the Heuneberg are impressive. But, it must be recognised that the number of items recovered is comparatively small in contrast to what was found in southern Gaul. There is no evidence to indicate either a constant flow of imported wares, or that the subsequent redistribution of these imports helped to maintain the Hallstatt political structure by generating local dependency (Figure 3.7). In fact, little evidence exists to demonstrate that anything but indigenous goods were redistributed from these Celtic strongholds. For instance, new forms of indigenous ceramics were found in the Heuneberg, all of which utilise new firing and decoration techniques. Many of these pots were mass-produced (Kimmig 1975, 56). This suggests that the vessels may have been produced to serve a larger community of customers and not just for local distribution. No evidence has of yet been found to substantiate the theory. Moreover, thousands of sites in Lorraine, Franche-Comté and Bourgogne demonstrate mining, smelting and smithing of iron (Leroy et al 2000). Conversely, no evidence for the exportation to the Mediterranean of other items, such as tin and slaves, has been found other than the "anachronistic extrapolations from much later periods" (Creed 2006, 60). This, in conjunction with the limited geographic distribution of the "spectacular" Mediterranean wares, supports the thought of a direct trade link between Celtic strongholds and Massaliote traders.

This brings us back to the quality and rarity of the items found at the above hillforts. Not only were these high-quality goods, but they were often produced in large dimensions in need of special methods of transport, which further demonstrates the high-status of the item. While no conclusive evidence exists, the existence of exceptional goods, such as the Vix krater, may support the idea of direct trade links and a concern for political and economic affiliation – the items may have been gifts and not necessarily manufactured for strictly trade purposes.

The disruptions in the fifth century and the ultimate collapse of the partnership between the Celtic hillforts and Massalia, therefore, cannot be attributed to one factor. Furthermore, the relationship of each of the major hillforts

(Vix, the Heuneberg, and Höhenasperg) to one another is as yet unresolved. Each of the élite cultures present are, nonetheless, relatively uniform. A comparison of the two populations would allow for a better interpretation of the relationship existing in the seventh to fifth centuries. It could also clarify more regional dynamics during the early iron age.

Chapter 4
Consumption, Production and Southern Gaul

4.1 Massaliote Influence in southern Gaul: the chora

Massalia has been referred to as a city without territory. This has generally been thought to mean that the extramural territory was secondary to the city itself. It becomes clear, however, that Massalia did have a chora: an extramural, rural territory that was governed by the city. After the segregation between the north/central region and southern Gaul, Massalia seems to have turned attention to is hinterland, founding the majority of its daughter and establishing trade relationships with them.

The topic of the Massaliote chora has been debated for years, producing numerous articles and books dedicated to its discussion[1] (Bats and Tréziny 1986; Dietler 1997, 285-287; Hansen and Nielsen 2004, 74-79; Morel 1995, 45-46). Regardless, the definition of the chora has grown continually more complex. It is easier to define the land "subject" to Massalia in terms of its spheres of influence: Massalia itself, the territory surrounding it, and its daughter colonies, each with its own hinterland placed in its immediate sphere. The Massaliote chora, therefore, could be directly influenced by the mother city itself, or indirectly through the secondary Massaliote establishments. As demonstrated above, chronological discontinuities do, in some instances, exist between the foundation of the colonies and the development of the indigenous settlements in the hinterland. This could potentially be an exhibition of colonial control.

The relationship between the "controlled" hinterland and Massalia would be one of supply and demand. Unfortunately, as described above, imports to Massalia probably consisted of raw materials which are consumed and do not readily preserve in the archaeological record. This relationship can therefore only be "observed" by the importation of Mediterranean goods and the adaptation by indigenous populations.

By the same token, production and manufacture would allow for a reconstruction of the ways in which Massalia and its chora interacted.

4.2 Indigenous Adoption

The southern Gallic people seem to have been little influenced by Massalia during the first few centuries of contact. There is little evidence to suggest the adoption of anything other than wine drinking: wine amphorae and associated drinking ceramics are abundant, while luxury objects are rare (Dietler 1997, 283; Brun 2004, 201). There is one major exception; ceramic production equipment and techniques, ie the potter's wheel and the closed draft kiln, were rapidly incorporated into the indigenous regime. Several new forms of pottery, combining indigenous and Greek traditions, begin to manifest (Dietler 1997, 299; Graham 2001, 39). These feed into two broad classificatory families: céramique claire and grey-momochrome. Significant regional variation within each group is present.

4.2.1 Pottery

Céramique claire

Céramique claire is the designation for a group of pottery types popular in Mediterranean France from the last quarter of the sixth century until the mid-third century BC (Eschallier 1991, 63). There are several common identifiable characteristics (Dietler 1997, 300; Eschallier 1991, 63); it is generally wheel-turned and composed of a very fine-grained fabric; a wide range of colours, yellow-beige to pink-ochre, were produced by oxidation during firing; wares are usually decorated with red or brown-ochre paint, although some are unpainted. More localised forms are also recognisable.

The derivative, Pseudo-Ionian ware, was popular in the lower Rhône basin and along the Cote d'Azur. These ceramics are classified as the tableware of Massalia, produced for both colonial and indigenous consumption. Numerous forms were produced by the Massaliotes. However, only certain items, mainly drinking cups, pitchers and small bowls, were exported to the indigenous population during the first century of contact (Dietler 1997, 300). By the mid-sixth century, Pseudo-Ionian drinking wares were being imitated in indigenous workshops.

Another variant was Rhodanian subgeometric. It was manufactured in indigenous workshops (Benoit 1965, 168-172) located in the lower Rhône Basin during the late sixth and fifth centuries. The elaborate decorations found on both Greco-Etruscan and indigenous forms are categorically definitive.

Western Languedoc and Roussilion were engaged in the

---

[1] Similarly, the *chora* and/or territories of several southern Gallic cities have also been extensively discussed: see Clavel-Lévêque and Mallart 1995; Clavel-Lévêque and Vignot 1998.

production of Ibero-Languedocian ware, another céramique claire variant (Jully and Nordstrom 1972; Solier 1976-1978). A detailed comparative study of these ceramics and their distribution was done by Gailledrat (1993a, b). He was able to identify four major production clusters: lower Hérault, lower Aude and Orb Valleys, and the Roussillon Plain. Each of these groups is thought to have represented local workshops, which seem to have been in operation during the late sixth century. By the fifth century, they were actively involved in the manufacturing of Ibero-Languedocian ceramics. Several series of Spanish imports were also identified.

Two large forms are prominent: jars, biconical or spherical vessels with an abrupt everted rim, and urns, long-necked, wide bodied vessels with an everted rim (Gailledrat 1993a). These ceramics are thought to have been used for either water-cooling or the brewing and storage of beer (see Michel et al 1992). However, physiochemical analysis has yet to be done.

Classification of céramique claire is still evolving (Benoit 1965, 168-172; Py 1971, 80-82; Eschallier 1991; Bats 1993; Dietler 1990, 229-261). It is difficult, however, to identify centres of production since only in Marseille have kilns and other archaeological traces been identified (Dietler 1997, 303). Distribution patterns, however, have pointed to several possible production areas: the Hérault Valley (Py 1990b, 551; 1993b), the region between the Cèze and Tave rivers in eastern Languedoc (Goury 1995) and, around the site of le Pegue in western Provence (Lagrand and Thalmann 1973). Recent studies have shown the production history around le Pegue is more complex than was originally thought (Eschallier 1991).

GREY-MONOCHROME

Grey-monochrome pottery is a family of hybrid-ceramics which developed in Mediterranean France during the sixth and fifth centuries (Arcelin-Pradelle 1984; Dietler 1990, 261-294; Nickels 1978; Py 1993c). It is classified as a wheel-thrown ceramic. Firing produces a reducing atmosphere, creating colours ranging from light grey to black monochrome. Decoration, when present, is incised and usually consists of a series of horizontal bands, wavy lines, or festoons made with comb or straight grooves (Dietler 1997, 302).

Initially, this group of ceramics was known as céramique phocéenee. They were originally believed to have been imported and distributed by Massalia from the eastern Mediterranean (Benoit 1965, 153-163; Jannoray 1955, 59-60; Villard 1960, 51-52). A comparative study done by Arcelin-Pradelle (1984; Arcelin-Pradelle et al 1982) considered the technical details and variety of forms from 87 sites in Provence and eastern Languedoc. Results indicated that almost all the pottery was locally produced. Patterns of distribution suggest probable regions of manufacture (see also Py 1990b, 544-547): Nickels identified areas of production for three separate groups in western Languedoc and Roussillon (1978; 1980). Similarly, Ugolini and Olive (1987-1988) identified one in Beziers. Furthermore, kiln wasters were found at the settlement of Mourre de Seve, Vaucluse (Arcelin-Pradelle 1984, 129, 146; Batut 1986).

Manufacturing and exportation of grey-monochrome ceramics began in Massalia no later than the second quarter of the sixth century BC. Evidence demonstrates that the majority of forms produced were derived from indigenous repertoires: over three-quarters of the all the recognisable grey-monochrome shards found belong to indigenous forms. Arcelin-Pradelle (1984, 145) concluded that grey-monochrome wares, therefore, were designed with the indigenous population in mind. With that in mind, it is interesting to note that imitation and production of grey-monochrome pottery began almost immediately in indigenous settlements of the lower Rhône Basin (Arcelin-Pradelle 1984). Workshops operating in the lower Hérault Valley are contemporary with those in Massalia (Houlès and Janin 1992, 435).

Regional preferences are evident (Arcelin-Pradelle 1984; Dietler 1990, 261-294; Nickels 1980; Py 1993c): in the Lower Rhône Basin, Greek forms significantly represented at indigenous settlements were wine pitchers and drinking cups. Conversely, the predominant form in production in western Languedoc and Roussilion was a wide-shallow bowl with a flat protruding lip derived from the Greek repertoire. While thousands of examples have been found in this region, only a handful of this form has been found in Provence (Arcelin-Pradelle 1984, 19; Nickels 1978).

Distribution of these wares is generally confined to Mediterranean France. However, several extant pieces of grey-monochrome wares have been discovered at Hallstatt sites in Burgundy, Jura, and western Switzerland (Feugère and Guillot 1986; Gaiffe 1985; Schwab 1982; Scotto 1985).

4.2.2 Wine and Oil

AMPHORAE

Massaliote amphorae are easily identified by their characteristic shape and fabric (Goudineau 1983, 77). The most common type, and the one of particular importance to this study, began to be produced as early as the sixth century BC. Although the form gradually evolved (Bertucchi 1992; Py 1978a; Wallon 1979), the shape and heavily micaceous fabric were maintained. These amphorae were preceded by forms using a feldspathic temper, and succeeded in the second century by forms with a recognisably non-micaceous fabric (Bertucchi 1982; 1983).

These common amphorae types were produced in Marseille, as is indicated by the archaeological remains of amphorae kilns (Conche 1996). Petrographic and chemical analyses indicate that amphorae were manufactured from local clays (Picon 1985; Reille 1985; Ricq-de Bouard 1985; Fillières 1978). Conversely, the micaceous component was imported from a source located 90km east along the coast. Analysis of the kiln wasters associated with the feldspathic amphorae demonstrates similar sourcing patterns (Reille and Abbas 1992).

Distribution is generally limited to Mediterranean France, although a few examples of amphorae have been found at late Hallstatt sites and early La Tène sites in temperate France, Switzerland, southern Germany and other areas of the western Mediterranean (Bats 1990c; Bertucchi 1992; Dietler 1990, 194-229; Lüscher 1996).

WINE AND OIL PRODUCTION

No evidence of wine or oil production has been found within the city of Marseille (Brun 2004, 204). Excavations at Saint-Jean-du-Desert, situated close to Marseille, reveal traced of vineyards dating between the fourth and second centuries BC (Boissinot 1995). Similar finds from Lattes indicate the gradual establishment of grape cultivation and wine production.

Remains of grape pips were identified at the site of Lattes (Buxó i Capdevila 1996). Although grapes were present during the fourth century BC (Buxó i Capdevila 1993), they were particularly abundant from the third century BC onwards. The increased presence of pips may suggest a change from use as a direct food source to cultivation for wine production (Buxó i Capdevila 1996, 404). Woodland clearance increased during two periods, 300-275 BC and 225-200 BC, possibly making more land available for cultivation (Chabal 1991). In co-ordination with the archaeobotanical data, a reduction in the number of imported amphorae, a corresponding rise in the number of dolia, containers possibly used for wine storage, during the third and second centuries (Buxo i Capdevila 1996, 404; Garcia 1992a, 173), and plantation trenches dating to the third and first centuries BC (Brun 2004, 206-207), further hint at the progressive development of wine production.[2]

Several other studies demonstrate similar patterns for early grape cultivation. At Gailhan (Erroux 1980a; 1987) and Marduel (Py 1990b; Marnival 1988), grapes were domestically grown in the sixth and fifth centuries BC,[3] while after the beginning of the fourth century, cultivation is regularly identified: Mauressip and Montjean begin cultivating in the fourth and third centuries BC, les Castels de Nages in the second century BC, followed by Cavaillon (Py 1990b), La Lagaste (Erroux 1980b), Canet-des-Marues (Py 1990b) and Ambrusson (Ruas 1989) in the first century BC.

Similar patterns can be discerned for oil production. Before the second century BC, there is some material possibly signifying oil production: troughs have been found in levels dating between the fourth and second centuries BC at Saint-Blaise (Brun 2004, 208) as well as a Martigues (Chausserie-Laprée and Nin 1987), and at Lattes in a third century context (Garcia 1992b, 238-239). During the second century, oil production seems to have intensified. This is attested at several indigenous sites where vestiges of lever presses and counterweights have been found (Brun 2004, 208): Baumajour, Baou de Saint-Marcel, Pierredon, la Courtine d'Oillioules, Glanum, Entremont (described above), and Lattes (Brun 1993, 308). Remnants of lever presses have also been discovered in Languedoc, but none of them were in situ. Several sites, including des Caisses (Mouriès), la Cloche, and Notre-Dame de Pitie, have yielded finds of olive stones. Both the domesticated varieties of indigenous olive and olives imported from the eastern Mediterranean Basin were represented (Terral 1997, 71; 2004).

No oil or wine presses dating to the pre-roman period have been identified within Massalia, although blocks and counterweights have been found at Olbia (Brun 2004, 204) and Agde (Garcia 1992b, 242-243). Likewise, a possible press and two counterweights were found at Condounèu (Verdin et al 1996-1997, 189-192), and blocks with central depressions akin to those found at Agde were found at Ensérune and Montfau (Garcia 1992b, 242-247). Evidence indicates that techniques of wine and oil pressing spread quickly to Celto-Ligurian territories. This is best illustrated by finds at Entremont (Figure 4.1) (Brun 2004, 207; Brun 1993, 310; Goudineau 1984, 220; Benoit 1968, 18-19), la Coutrine d'Oillioules (Layet 1949a, b) and Mouriès.

At Entremont, fifteen presses, eight troughs, and seven counterweights have been found. All of these were associated with oil, and maybe wine, production (Brun, Charriere, and Congès 1998). Several of these were found either in situ or slightly displaced within the site (Benoit 1968, 18). One of these was decorated with herringbone patterns akin to those found on the ramparts of Saint-Blaise, Olbia, constructions at Glanum, and the "Wall of Crinas" at Marseille (discussed below). Goudineau (1984) has concluded that the similarities in decoration must mean direct Massaliote involvement (discussed below).

4.3 Consumption, Production and Massalia

The rapid adoption of foreign pottery technologies demonstrates a new and different process by which indigenous settlements were supplied with foreign goods. Unlike importation, local manufacture of goods introduces material costs: permanent workshops were built and fitted with equipment such as kilns, wheels, clay purification tanks and storage facilities (Dietler 1997, 299). Furthermore, these new technologies would have required new skills of production. This transformed the indigenous pottery systems from a household to a workshop industry. In the lower Rhône this process is linked to an increased demand for tableware (Dietler 1997, 299). The second and first centuries BC are signified by the introduction of new forms of hybrid ceramics and a change in the economy of ceramic production. The indigenous workshops of the Massaliote hinterland produced Greek forms of cooking vessels with hand-modelled techniques to supply the colonial city of Massalia (Arcelin 1993b).

Massaliote fine ware, however, is found in abundance within the city itself and at its daughter colonies. Kilns and

---

[2] See also Py and Buxó i Capdevila 2001.
[3] For other sites see Bouby and Marnival 2001 and Boissinot 2001.

Figure 4.1: (A) Olive press counterweight found at Entrement (B) Olive press found at Entremont

kiln wasters have been found in the city, although evidence indicates that production took place at several different locations throughout its history (Benoit 1965; Bertucchi 1982; Bertucchi et al 1995; Conche 1996; Gantès 1992a). Massalia also engaged in the manufacture of imitation Attic wares from the last quarter of the fifth century until the last quarter of the fourth century (Py 1978b; 1993d). At most indigenous sites, however, imported fine wares account for only a marginal per cent of the total pottery assemblage until at least the beginning of the second century BC. Such is the case at Nages (Py 1978c, 69) and Gailhan (Dedet 1980). The majority of the assemblages are comprised of indigenous forms of ceramics which were locally produced (Bats 1988a, 228-229; Eschallier 1991). Likewise, Massaliote pottery accounts for less than fiver per cent of the pottery assemblage on any indigenous site in the third and second centuries BC (Goudineau 1983).

Other ceramic imports are found on indigenous settlements, though not well-represented. For instance, Megarian Bowls,[4] various ceramics from Greece and Asia Minor (Bats 1979, 163-164; 1988a, 148-150), and those from Iberia were relatively late and scarce. The one exception is Campanian pottery. Ceramics from the workshops of petites estampilles,[5] and Campanian A from Magna Graecia were discovered in greater numbers (Morel 1978). Unfortunately, none of these can be successfully proven to have been imported and distributed through Massalia (Villard 1960, 128ff; Gallet de Santerre 1977, 33-57).

Massaliote amphorae demonstrate similar patterns (Goudineau 1983; Bats 1988a, 229). On any site, the total number of amphorae from the sixth and fifth centuries is much greater than that of the Hellenic period. If the periods are studied more closely, it becomes evident that there are certain patterns which can be found in the Vaunage (nr. Nimes). First, Marseille had a monopoly on wine distribution in central Gaul until the third century BC (Brun 2004, 201). By the second century, remains of Republican amphorae indicate an increased preference for Italian wine. Italian wine importation is, therefore, thought to have replaced Massaliote wine (Loughton 2003; Py 1990b, 841; Brun 2004, 201-202). By 100 BC, it is completely replaced (Goudineau 1983). After the Roman conquest, Italian and Sicilian wine imports increased exponentially in southern and central Gaul (Tchernia 1983; Goudineau 1983).

Conversely, Massalia does not seem to ever have been involved in the production of its own wine and oil.[6] The Greeks may not even have introduced the local indigenous population to grape vine (see Planchais 1982) or its cultivation for consumption. Archaeological and botanical evidence indicates that cultivation started in the first iron age in southern Gaul (Marinval 1988), including at Le Marduel (Chabal 1982) and La Jouffe. It remains unclear as to whether or not local production of wine began at the same time. Furthermore, grapes may have been cultivated for direct consumption (Andre 1981; Marnival 1988), and only later, used for wine. The bi-products and wastes from both processes, ie pips and skins, would have been used secondarily as fuel.

Aside from the press, the only other material evidence of wine-making is dolia. Direct evidence demonstrating their association in wine and oil storage has yet to be found. Small finds have alluded to the practice of viticulture and oleiculture: a grape pruning knife from Nages (Py 1990b), stamp-marks of grapes on indigenous dolia at Ensérune (Jannoray 1955, 262-263), and symbols related to vine cultivation at Montlaurès (Marnival 1988).

4.4 Implications for the role of Massalia

When considering patterns of production and consumption, it quickly becomes evident that the role of Massalia changed. Initially founded as an emporion, it quickly became reliant on its chora. The indigenous settlements became increasingly involved in the production and supply of goods to the colonial city as well as to other settlements in the area. This is evidenced in the pottery assemblages: Massaliote pottery and other fine wares (with the exception of Campanian ceramics) comprise a very small percentage of the total. Although some sites demonstrate high percentages, most of these are sites that are located proximally to daughter colonies and, ultimately, demonstrate deterred development (see chapter 1). Until the second century when there seems to have been an increased demand for imported Italian wine, even the number of amphorae on sites is low. Similarly, the vestiges of production on indigenous sites demonstrate a decreased dependence on Massalia.

The lack of Hellenic goods and practices is clearly seen when considering Celtic sites. Gallic forms of ceramics are still being produced locally for the indigenous population. Grey-monochrome ware, originally thought to have been Massaliote made, demonstrates a consideration of Gallic appeal. This perhaps signifies a more conscious approach to the indigenous population by the inhabitants of Massalia, than an indigenous desire to partake in Hellenic practices. Furthermore, much of this production, especially in terms of oil and possibly wine, was carried out at sites that were not under Massaliote control.

---

[4] A Greek hemi-spherical ceramic vessel which may or may not have a low ring foot. The outside of the bowl is generally covered in ornamental reliefs (Cook 1997, 204-205; Rotroff 1978).

[5] A black-glazed pottery thought to have been produced in Rome. The most common form is black-glazed, hemi-spherical bowls decorated with stamped motifs. Decorations are generally found in the centre or along the rim (Bats 1976; Castanyer, Sanmarti and Tremoleda 1993; Morel 1969; Py 1976)

[6] See Bouby and Marnival 2001 for a discussion of the possible role of Massalia in the stimulus for indigenous grape cultivation. Grape pips have been found in the place Jules Verne in Marseille (Bouby and Marnival 2001, 24-25) possibly suggesting local viticulture. However, aside from the production of amphorae, no other evidence of wine presses or grape cultivation have been found.

CHAPTER 5
URBANISM IN SOUTHERN GAUL

5.1 Late iron age culture

Native sites in southern Gaul (Figure 5.1) were not drastically affected by the Hallstatt – La Tène transition. Instead, many of their bronze age Urnfield, Iberian, or Ligurian characteristics were maintained (Sanders 1957, 17, 350). On the coastal plains surrounding Massalia, the fusion of the Hallstatt culture and these older traditions created a new culture – the Celto-Ligurians. This new culture was also able to retain its individuality against La Tène (Green 1989, 10; Drinkwater 1983, 10) and, initially, Greek influence. However, the indigenous population ultimately began to display Hellenistic characteristics within several components of every-day life, such as art (discussed below), architecture, and urbanism.

5.2 Iron age changes in hillfort and settlement construction

The year-round temperate climate produced arable agricultural soils, allowing a relatively stable but dense population to be sustained during the first millennium BC (Cunliffe 1988, 39; Barruol 1969). In eastern Provence, settlements were small and characterized by rock-cut shelters and the use of caves.[1] Conversely, western Languedoc and the coastal areas of the lower Rhône displayed small and scattered hamlets and villages (Dedet et al 1985; Prades et al 1985). Most of these settlements, however, were confined to the edges of coastal lagoons. Internal areas demonstrate an assortment of rock dwellings, caves, and more defensive hilltop sites. These differential settlement patterns have been used to support the idea of a cultural divide among the southern Gallic Celts, the boundary of which would have run along the river Rhône. Despite this cultural division, domestic units were of fairly uniform construction: one room, wattle-and-daub, post-frame structures. Although some organisation must have existed, it is difficult to quantify. The houses seem to be haphazardly arranged without regard to any organisational criteria (Dietler 1997, 310).

As the early iron age progressed, it was accompanied by various changes in settlement construction. Although considerable regional and individual variation is apparent, several characteristics can be recognised on a wider geographic scale.[2] These include changes in fortification, building material, and organisation of settlements.

In the last half of the fifth century, more fortified hilltop sites were built and most lowland sites were surrounded by defensive circuits (Arcelin and Dedet 1985; Py 1990b). The majority of these settlements were between one and ten hectares, and densely spread over the landscape. In the mid and lower Hérault Valley, conversely, they were found every 10km and could encompass a territory of 20sq km (Garcia 1993, 1995; Garcia and Orliac 1993).

Stone construction was generally reserved for funerary monuments or for terracing projects. Any ramparts were built of earth and timber, although the fortification of settlements was rare in Mediterranean Gaul during the late bronze and very early iron age. It is interesting to note that the sites which were fortified around the mid-sixth century, ie Saint-Blaise and Les Baou des Noirs (Latour 1985), were located in the lower Rhône Basin. L'Arquet, Tamaris, and Saint-Pierre-lès-Martiques, along with other settlements located near the coast, received defensive circuits slightly later, during the first half of the sixth century (Arcelin et al 1983; Bouloumié 1984; Lagrand 1959; 1979; 1981; 1986). Fortification construction varied. Some walls were made of dry stone walls with fill, sometimes using double or triple construction, and initially with few towers.[3]

Internally, the wattle-and-daub post-frame houses gradually gave way to stone foundations with mud-brick or earthen walls. The earliest examples, dating between the mid-sixth and fifth centuries BC, are found at Saint Blaise (Bouloumié 1979, 232), Le Cros (Gasco 1994), L'Agréable (Gallia 1985, 394), and Plan de la Tour (Dedet 1990). Irregularly placed, one room, oval-shaped huts were subsequently abandoned and replaced by rows of similarly-oriented rectangular houses.[4] These were also single-room units roughly 10-25

---

[1] Gorges du Verdon (Lagrand 1987), grotte du chambers d'Alaric (*Gallia Préhistoire* xv 1972, 515-516; Guilaine and Ayme 1960, 145-146), grotte du Lierre (Gagnière and Granier 1962), grotte des Planches (Audouze and Buchsenschutz 1991, 125; Pétrequin et al 1985), and grotte du Hasard (*Gallia Préhistoire* xv 1972, 530-533). See also Gallet de Santerre 1964, 504 and Lagrand 1968.

[2] This is true of both southern Gaul as a region, and within the wider context of Gaul. For this wider context see Büchsenschütz 1995; Collis 1984.

[3] The presence of towers is problematic, see pages 57-58. For an overview of the region, see Arcelin and Dedet 1985.

[4] For a general discussion see Dietler 1997, 315. For specific sites – Montlaures: *Gallia* 1960, 616; 1964, 479-480; Giry 1962, 159-173; 1962, 76-88. Saint-Laurent de Carnos: Charmasson 1967, 145-168; Barruol 1969, 409. Vie-Cioutat: *Gallia* 1969, 405; 1971, 393. Mauressip: Barruol 1969, 408; *Gallia* 1971, 397-399; *Ecole antique de Nimes* 3, 1969, 39-91. Saint-Vincent-de-Gaujac: Gallet de Santerre 1964, 500. Dedet (1999) gives a very discussion of construction trends and social implications in Languedoc oppida between the late sixth and late first centuries BC.

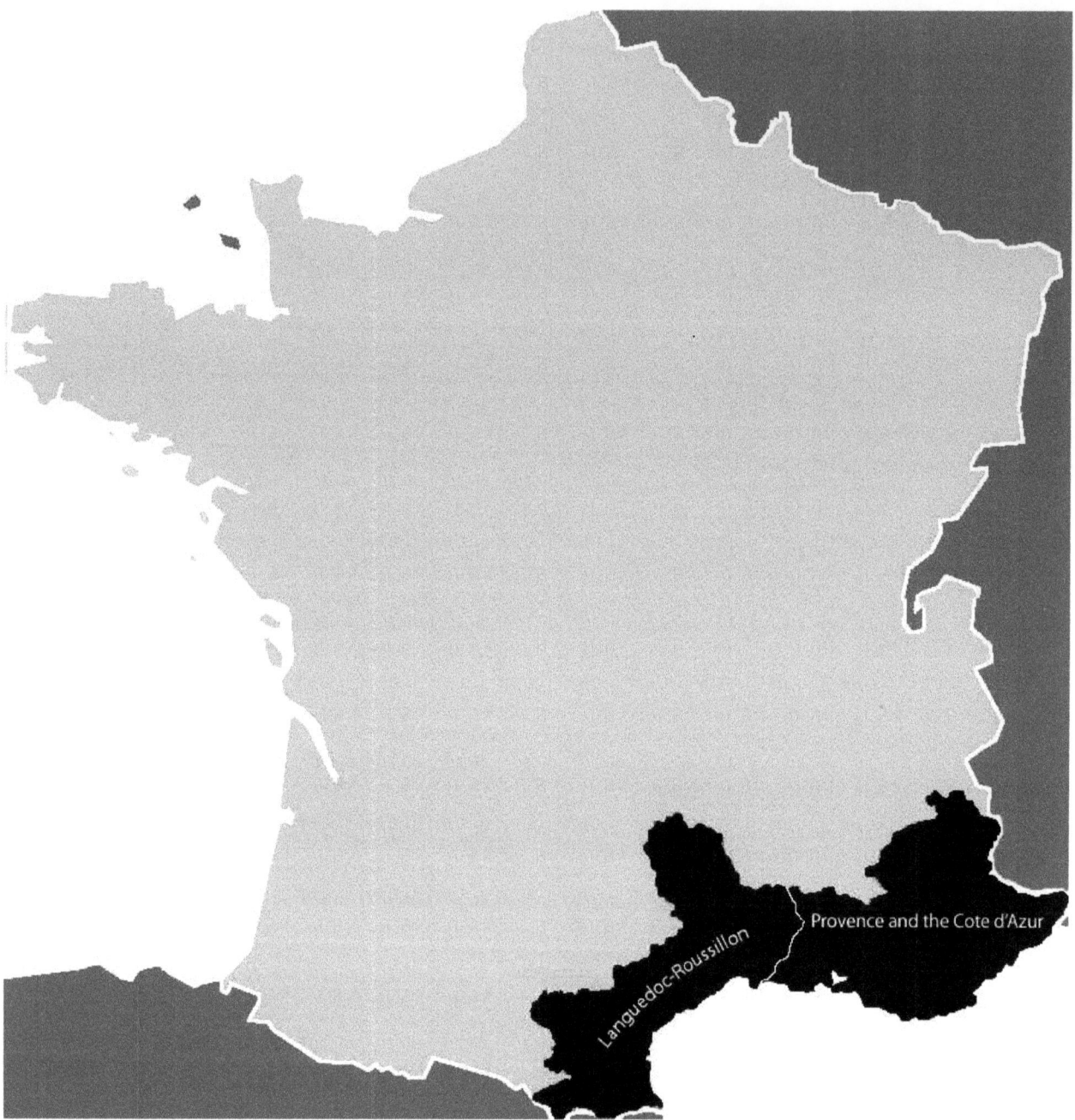

Figure 5.1: Map of general area of study

sqm in size. By the last half of the fifth century, multi-room houses were being constructed in western Languedoc (Dedet 1987; Michelozzi 1982; Py 1990b). Similarly, there is some evidence potentially indicating the construction of two-storey buildings at Entremont (Arcelin 1992a; 1992b, 321; 1993b; Py 1996a). Although these features were primarily attested on larger hilltop sites (see below), some lowland sites display the same features.[5]

Albeit rare, early Graeco-Italic houses have been found in western Languedoc (Py 1990b, 127). These peristyle courtyard residences were organised on a grid either in rows with intervening narrow streets or in back-to-back blocks.

Similarly, houses with apsidal ends were found in Gard at Gailhan (Dedet 1990) and in Hérault at La Monédière (Dedet 1990, 47; Nickels 1976). These styles are usually late developments and specifically found in the lower Rhône Valley (Py 1996a, Roth Congès 1992a-c).

5.3 Changes in settlement patterns

As stated above, settlement patterns had varied throughout southern Gaul. The most drastic differences are readily identifiable from one side of the Rhône to the other. As the iron age developed, so too did the social, economic, and political situations. This is reflected in the changing settlement patterns during the fourth to second centuries BC. Again, each section of southern Gaul demonstrated its own characteristic settlement type and expressed a different pattern of changes (Arcelin 2004; Fevrier 1973, 9-11).

---

[5] See Lattes (Barruol et al 1988; Chazelles and Roux 1988; Garcia 1990; 1994; Py 1989; 1990c; 1996b), Arles (Arcelin 1987; 1990, 194-201) and l'Ile (Chausserie-Laprée and Nin 1987; 1990; Chausserie-Laprée et al 1984).

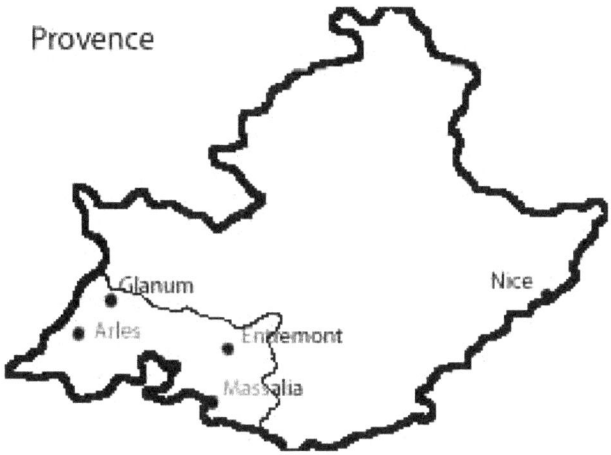

Figure 5.2: Map of Provence and indigenous sites of importance to this study

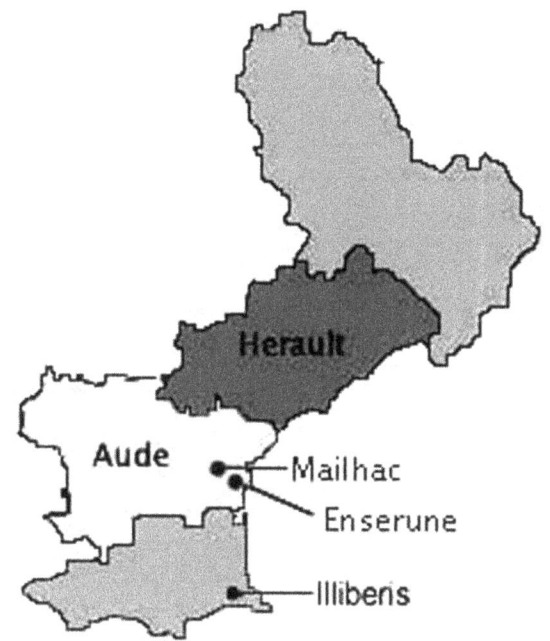

Figure 5.3: Map of Languedoc-Roussillon and indigenous sites of importance to this study

In the Massaliote hinterland of Provence (Figure 5.2), the fourth and third centuries BC were characterised by the abandonment of the lowlands. Dispersed farmsteads were abandoned, and small (<1ha) hilltop villages began to appear. These were mostly agricultural settlements. By the late third and early second centuries BC, these sites were destroyed, usually violently, and subsequently deserted (Dietler 1997, 317). Larger hilltop settlements, upwards of 6ha in size, began to be reconstructed and expanded. This indicates a growth in population, perhaps stimulated by an influx of people from the abandoned agricultural villages (Woolf 1998, 108). The original settlement at Entremont, for instance, received new ramparts, and a new "lower town" was constructed (see below). This new section, displayed the development of multi-room houses (as discussed above) and an artisan quarter with kilns (Benoit 1975, 236). Other sites, such as Pierredon and l'Ile demonstrate similar extensions of the primary settlement. Around the same time, fortifications were elaborated and monumental public spaces, such as sanctuaries (see below), were built (Dietler 1997, 317-8). After the Roman conquest of 123 BC, most of these were destroyed or abandoned and small lowland settlements began to reappear (Arcelin and Tréziny 1990).

Conversely, there is no indication that eastern Languedoc and Roussillon (Figure 5.3) experienced the same destruction or instability during the second century. Large fortified hilltop settlements established in the previous period seem to have continued to develop (Nickels 1983; Py 1990b). A few large sites appear to have housed the bulk of the population during the fourth and third centuries BC (Garcia 1995). Illiberis, for example, grew to 10ha in size. Little evidence has been produced to indicate that the countryside was occupied at all. During the second century BC, Illiberis seems to have decreased in size and small isolated sites were established in the countryside (Dietler 1997, 319). Similarly, the population in Corbières (lower Aude Valley) and along the coast in the second and third centuries BC was sparse. For the most part, the population was gathered into large settlements such as Ensérune, Cayla de Mailhac, and Montlauriès (Maune and Chazelles 1997, 187-189). After the Roman occupation during the mid-second century BC, many of these settlements rapidly went into decline and were abandoned by the mid first century BC (Dietler 1997, 319). This may have been caused by the foundation and expansion of the Roman colonies of Narbonne and Béziers.

5.4 Indigenous sites and urban development

5.4.1 Ensérune

Even though Ensérune is located on the top of an elongated ridge with sharp slopes on every side, the site is not isolated; there was access to antique trade routes such as the Garonne route, the Heraklean Road (Jannoray 1955, 37), and those leading through the Carcassonne Gap. Occupation is attested as early as the sixth century BC, but it was not until c. 425-220 BC (the period marked as Ensérune II) that any indication of urban structure can be witnessed.

Two types of houses were present: those made of stone on dry-stone foundations, and mud-brick domiciles with timber and earth roofs. All of these units were organised on a grid, albeit unusually, in long rows or on terraces. This is probably due to the odd shape of the site (Figure 5.4). Each row contained approximately twelve houses with one side fronting on a road. Earlier structures on the southern slope were replaced in the third century BC by terraced houses. Others were elaborated with tiled roofs, crudely carved capitals, and stucco facing.[6] Each house contained a dolia or silo. Although the site had a spring, which is still flowing today, it is questionable as to whether or not

---

[6] Although constructions at Ensérune included more elaborate details, the architecture was more modest and rudimentary than what is revealed in the remains at Glanum. For more details see Jannoray 1955.

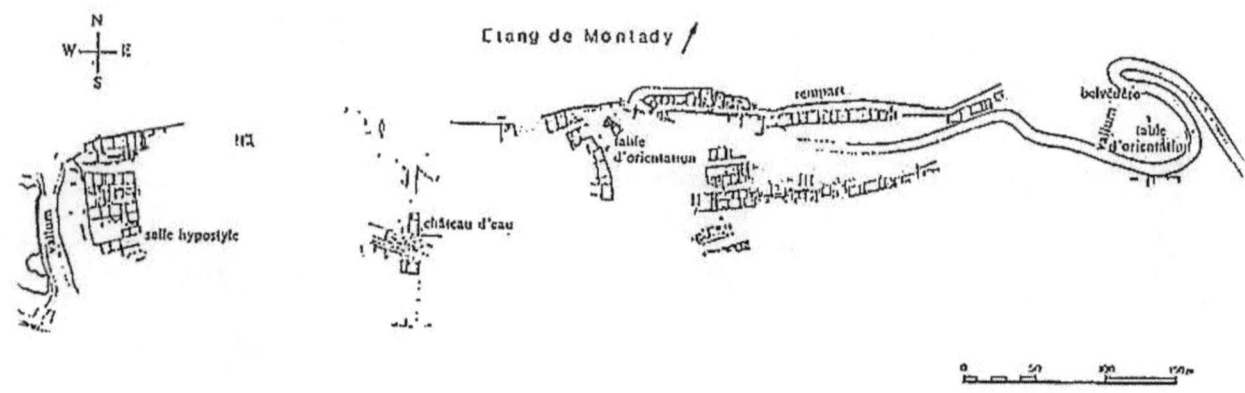

Figure 5.4: Plan of Enserune

it provided enough water to sustain the population. If it did not, it would explain the elaborate system of silos and cisterns (Gallet de Santerre 1980); a terrace was constructed near the centre of the settlement which interconnected forty-five cisterns enabling them to store a total of one million litres of water. An east-west road was also established.

In the late third century BC, Ensérune reached its largest extent and had an associated external settlement (Giry 1974, 10; Schwaller 1991, 360). The fortifications were rebuilt and the old cemetery was reused for new construction. No new necropolis seems to have been established. Except for the sanctuary, there is little evidence of any public buildings at any time. Following the destruction of the site in 220 BC, an extensive rebuilding project allowed the site to be reoccupied. No public architecture was included among the new constructions. The site was finally destroyed and abandoned after 100 AD (Jannoray 1955).

5.4.2 Saint Blaise

Saint Blaise (Figure 5.5) occupies a 5.5ha plateau between the Etang de Citis and the Etang de Lavalduc (Rolland 1951, 7, 17). A small settlement seems to have been established in the area before the seventh century BC. Its presence is indicated by small finds of lithic tools, flints and imported Bucchero, Etruscan, Corinthian and Attic ceramics (Rolland 1949, 6; Bouloulmié and Borély 1992, 16-17; Arcelin 1971, 11-12, 81). No associated structures have been found. It is not until Saint Blaise III (625-475 BC) that the official site was founded.

During this phase, the site was fitted with irregular stone houses, streets, and a roughly-trimmed rampart (Rolland 1956) situated on the least defensive side of the plateau. Unfortunately, the archaeological record is not completely intact: the archaeological transition usually passes directly from Saint-Blaise III to Saint-Blaise V, the "Hellenic" phase lasting from 200 to the first half of the first century BC. As a result Saint-Blaise IV (475-200 BC) is usually referred to as "sub-archaic." Despite numerous excavations, only one house from this period has been identified (Bouloumié and Borély 1992, 17; Gateau and Provost 1996, 301).

There are several theories which attempt to explain the lack of continuity. First, the inhabitants of Saint-Blaise III may have occupied a reduced area compared to that of the final settlement. Second, at the end of the third century BC, the site was levelled and rebuilt. A main north-south thoroughfare was installed, and stone and mortar houses were arranged on a grid system (Bouloumié and Borély 1992, 17-18, 20-21, 25). Burned wood in sondage MN11 may indicate the burning and/or raising of existing structures in preparation for the reconstruction of the settlement on a planned layout (Bouloumié 1979, 232).

There is some indication that Saint-Blaise had a defensive curtain as early as the second half of the sixth century BC (Février 1973, 12). However, the construction of the later ramparts is more pertinent to this discussion. Several literary sources allude to the construction of Hellenistic ramparts around Saint-Blaise as early as the fourth century (Diodorus XIV, 42, 43, 50; XVI, 74 cf. Elian Var. Hist. VI, 12; Lafaye Dict. Des Ant. Gr. And Rom. IV, 363; Festus Avienus Ora Maritima, v. 701). There is much debate on the precise dating of the fortifications, but most scholars agree they must date between the fourth and second centuries BC (Rolland 1951, 45; Tréziny 1985).

The ramparts are of high-quality craftsmanship with evidence of skilled stone work, and the use of mortar. There are several other building elements and details demonstrated in the ramparts which have been used as evidence in the direct involvement of the Greeks (Rolland 1951, 126-127). Juxtaposed joints (Rolland 1956, 12), joints "a crochet," the intermediary wedging of smaller stones, and the presence of mason's marks (Benoit 1966, 16; Rolland 1951, 93) are construction techniques used in many Hellenic ramparts (Rolland 1956, 12; Bessac 1980). The stones in the west wall are dressed with herringbone patterns (Rolland 1951, 93). These herringbone decorations and mason's marks (Figure 5.6) are also present at Glanum (Rolland 1958, 91, and pl. 32), Olbia, the "Wall of Crinas" at Massalia (Figure 5.7) (Benoit 1966, 17), and on stone olive presses at Entremont (see Figure 4.1a and b) (Goudineau 1984, 119-220). This has been suggested as evidence for Greek construction because both Olbia and Massalia were

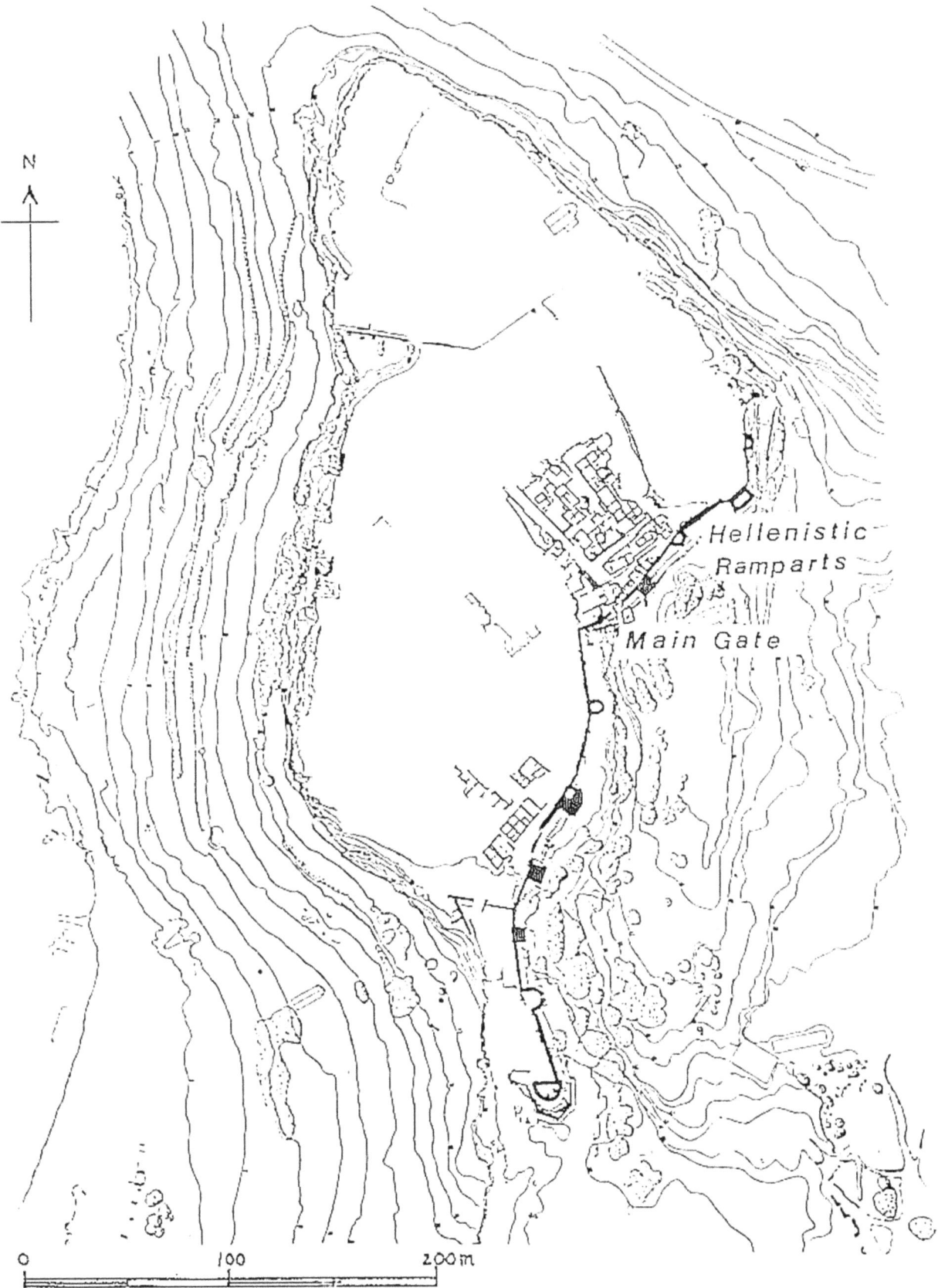

Figure 5.5: Settlement plan of Saint-Blaise

Culture Contact in Southern Mediterranean France

Figure 5.6: Herringbone stone-cuts on the fortification wall of Saint-Blaise

Figure 5.7: The Wall of Crineas, Marseille

Figure 5.8: Glanum

established as Greek colonies and not built upon earlier indigenous settlements. Herringbone decoration has also been found at Tarente and Corinth (CIG XIV 2422, 2423), further stimulating debate of Greek involvement.

Even though only a small portion of the site has been excavated, certain elements become noticeable: like Ensérune, there are no public or monumental buildings, the streets are organised on a "rough grid-plan," and the road is unpaved. The sanctuary demonstrates the observance of the Celtic Head Cult (discussed below). Like Entremont, Roquepertuse, and Ensérune, pillars with skull niches and over forty round-headed stelae have been discovered. As the stelae were reused in the rampart, their original placement cannot be ascertained (Rolland 1951, 41-46).

5.4.3 Glanum

Although Glanum was finally destroyed during the Germanic invasions of 270 AD (Wiseman 1998, 14), this discussion will be confined to the pre-Roman period. This period encompasses the evolution of the site from the sixth century until it's the official fall of Massalia in 49 BC (Charles-Picard 1963, 112).

Glanum is an interesting site which does not display the same characteristics or development as other indigenous settlements. Celto-Ligurian settlements were typically situated on top of high, defensive ground. It was not until the annexation of the province of Narbonensis and the declaration of the Pax Romana, that the hilltop settlements were abandoned for less defensive, valley bottom positions. After the collapse of the Roman Empire, these valley sites were abandoned and hilltops resettled. In light of this information, it is interesting that Glanum seems to have been established in the sixth century BC at the bottom of a valley gorge (Figure 5.8) (Février 1973, 13).

The city itself is a v-shaped area with one road, oriented north-south, entering through the gateway of the defensive wall (Figure 5.9) (discussed below). No grid plan is discernable because there are no cross-streets. On the west side of the site are stairs which allow access to the sanctuary. Despite its militarily weak position, a defensive wall was constructed. Although precise dating is impossible, Rolland (1958, 91) suggests a fourth-second century date (discussed below). The wall is 25m long, with one gateway, and is facing the sanctuary. This wall does not present a serious obstacle to any planned or determined attack; it protects only the sanctuary, leaving the residential portion of the city vulnerable. Recent studies have shown that the town was surrounded by a larger defensive network situated on the top of the surrounding hills (Augusta-Boularot 2004, 27-30). Consequently, this wall probably was a delimitation and not for defence.

Due to its location proximal to several trade routes, Glanum was continually influenced by economic contact with Massalia, Etruria, Iberia, and Italy. It was not until

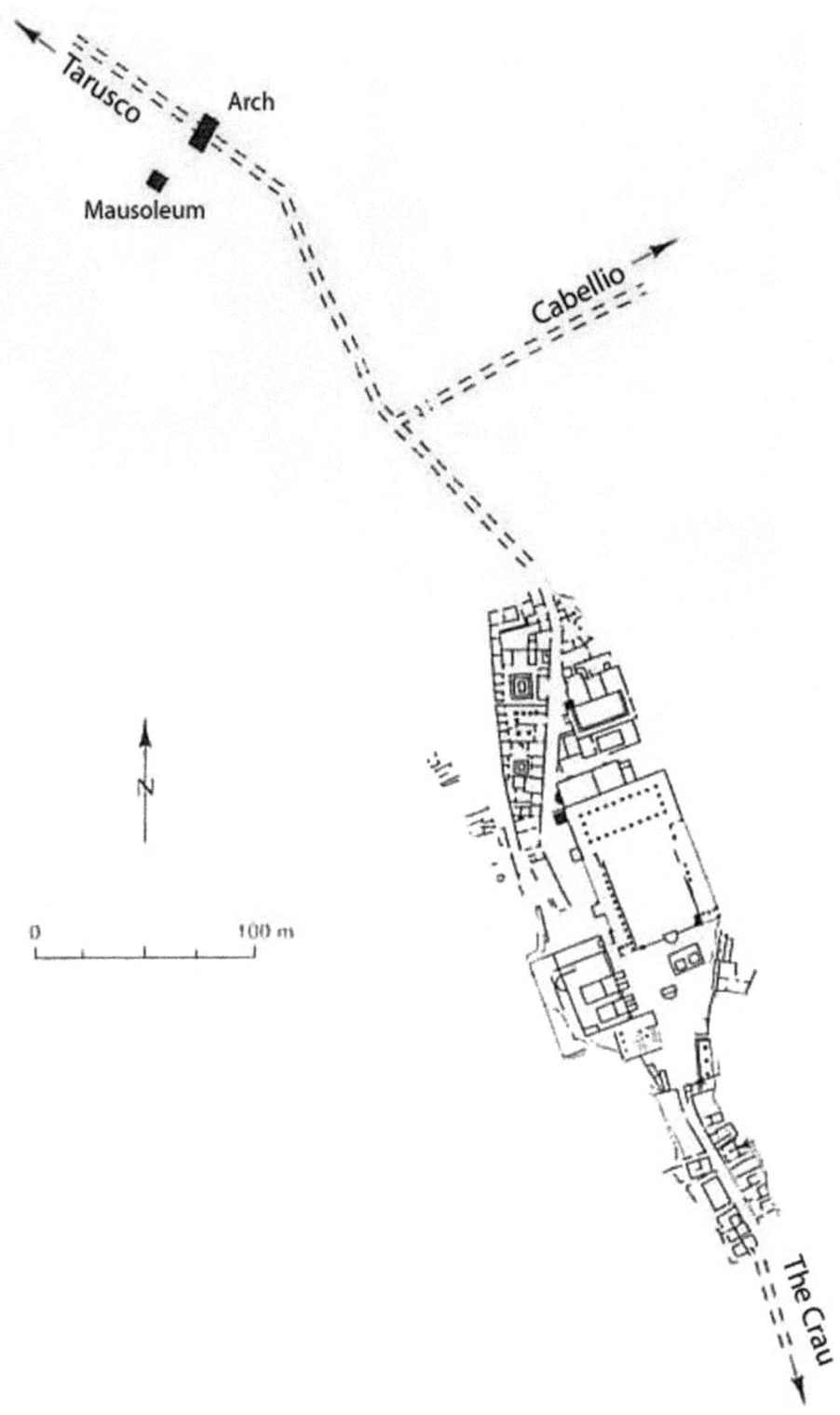

Figure 5.9: Settlement plan of Glanum

the second century[7] (Rolland 1946, 34-39; Charles-Picard 1963, 112), however, that the settlement was equipped with classically-inspired public buildings (Figure 5.10): a "bouleuterion" was constructed overlooking a small agora, and a trapezoidal "prytaneion" (Roth Congès 2000; 50-51) was decorated with eleven 4-figured capitals (Figure 5.11) depicting both Greek and indigenous mythology. A Tuscan temple with a dromos and stairway leading to a well and its associated tholos was also established (Roth Congès 2000, 50-51; CAG 13/2, no 100, 58). However, regardless of the Greek-inspired constructions, influence of the indigenous population can still be witnessed.

The sanctuary is located next to the "bouleuterion" and accessed by a staircase. As is indicated by Massaliote

---

[7] For more detailed information of building chronology see Rolland 1946, 34-39; dating information concerning the *bouleuterion* and the capitals, *Gallia* 1969, 434-446; and *Comptes rendus de l'Académie des inscriptions et Belles-Lettres* 1968, 105. For later archaeological developments, see Gros and Varène 1984.

Urbanism in Southern Gaul

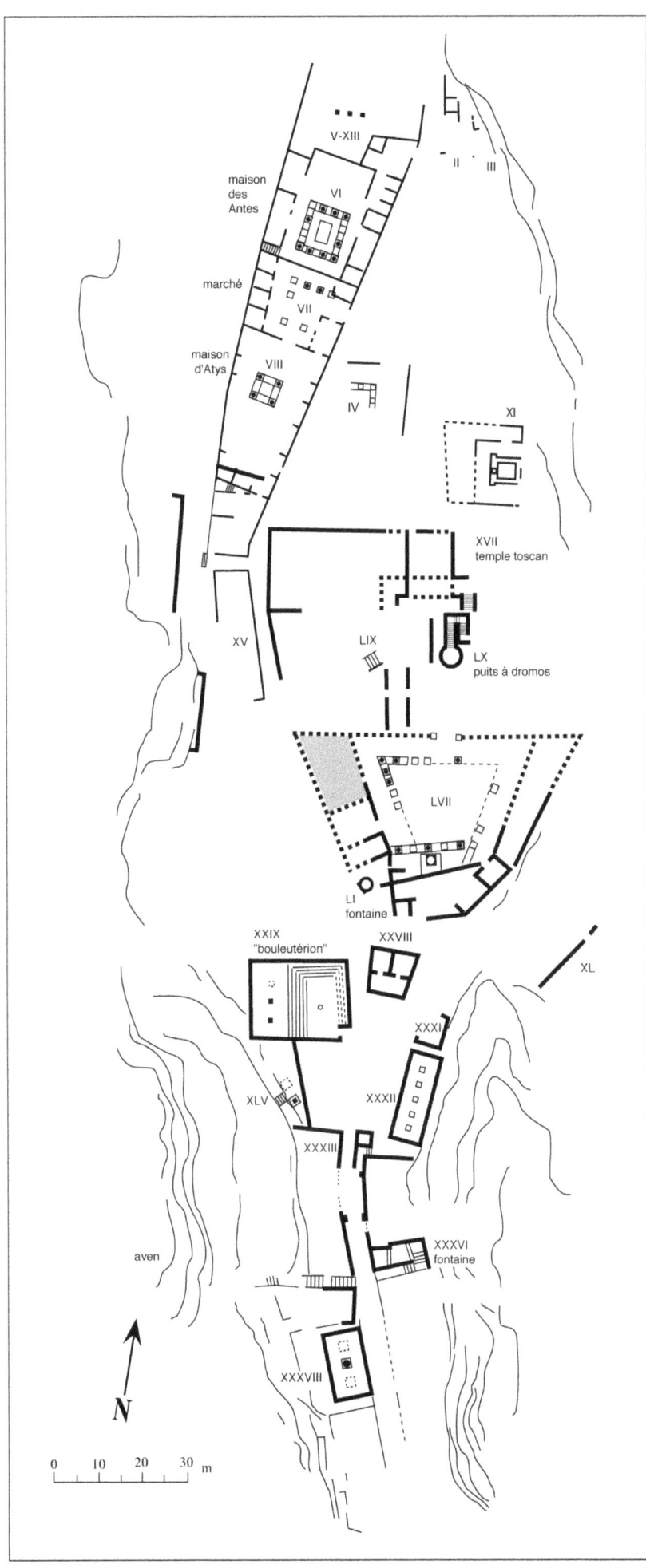

Figure 5.10: Plan of the monumental centre of Glanum in the 2nd century BC

Figure 5.11: Four-sided capitals found in the prytaneum in Glanum

coins and Ionian, Phocaean, and Attic ceramic shards, the sanctuary and the associated terraces were in use from at least the sixth century BC (Rolland 1958, 80, 87; Rolland 1936, 36-42). It was still in use during the second century and contained a shrine with indigenous statuary including accroupis, têtes coupées (see next chapter), lintels with head niches, and reliefs of horses (Roth Congès 1997; 2000, 5). To the south of the fortification wall, the sacred spring was protected by an overlaying building containing a staircase composed of large stone slabs leading down to the spring itself. A statue, epigraphically described as Matrebo Glaneikabo (RIG I, G-64), is dated to c. 100 BC and depicts a woman with a hood, earrings, and a torc.

The main street was paved and the residential quarter was fitted with six peristyle houses (Fabre 1934); many were decorated with mosaic floors, painted stucco and Corinthian pilasters (Rolland 1958, 120-123; Rolland 1946, 39). The number of porticoes and the length of adjacent sides vary from house to house (Rolland 1946, 38). After the destruction of the site in 125 BC, many of the public buildings, ie the "prytaneion," were destroyed and replaced by elaborate domiciles. Several theories attempt to explain the reason for Glanum's wealth; these include transhumance and its prestige as a religious site (Roth Congès 1997). Classification remains difficult (discussed in chapter 6).

Irrespective of the reasons behind its source of affluence and its complex urban development (Clerc 1930; Benoit 1945), it is clear that Glanum still possessed a local identity which is distinctly Celtic. Although equipped with the public buildings synonymous with a Greek colony, several characteristics, such as the sanctuary, religious statuary, and monolithic pillars, are akin to those found at Nîmes, La Cloche, Roquepertuse, and Entremont (Arcelin 1990). As a result, Glanum produced a level of Gallo-Greek syncretism not seen elsewhere.

5.4.4 Entremont

Entremont was the capital of the Salluvii, and was situated at the intersection of two roads: an east-west road linking Italy and Spain, and a southerly road leading to the Greek colony of Massalia (Benoit 1975, 227; Benoit 1957). It occupies a plateau 365m high, bounded by steep slopes to the south-east, south-west, and a gentler one to the north. The north and east sides of the site are protected by a defensive wall. Only the base, composed of poorly cut large square blocks on top of projecting foundations, is preserved. The ground surface does not seem to have been levelled prior to construction. Square towers were spaced every 19m along the wall. Unfortunately, the combination of chronological problems, several phases of rebuilding,

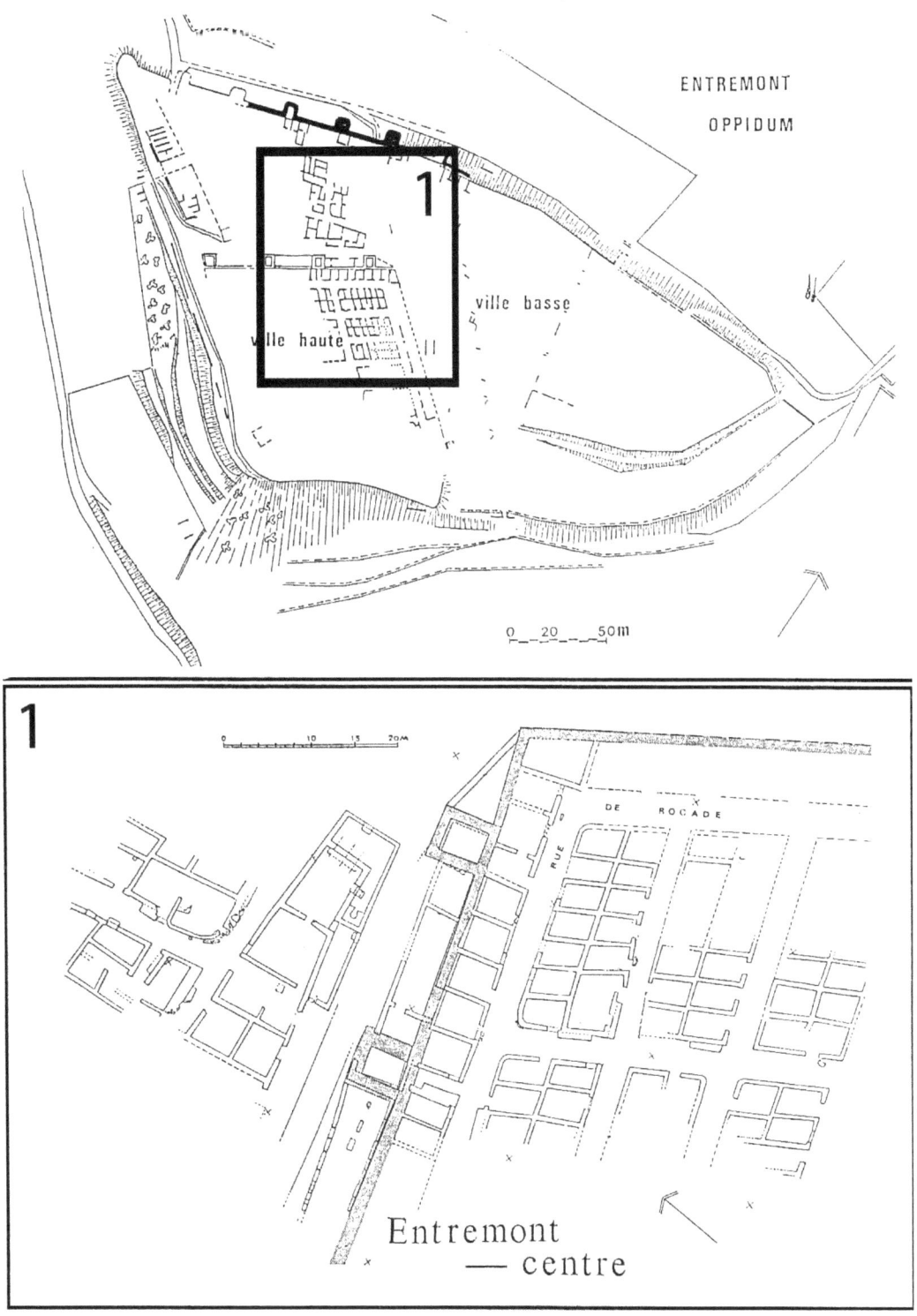

Figure 5.12: Site plans of Entremont (Hodge 1988, 198, 114 and 115)

and the modern military occupation of the site makes it difficult to provide a precise date for these defences. They are roughly attributed to the sixth to fourth centuries BC.

The second phase of the site (Entremont II) is dated between the fourth and third centuries BC. Large houses and a colonnaded building, identified as the sanctuary (discussed below), were built in the spaces between towers. Stelae from the sanctuary were reused in the construction,

as was material collected from the plateau itself (Benoit 1975, 233). The western slope was terraced in order to accommodate an external settlement. Houses were typically rock-cut and contained clay hearths (Benoit 1975, 236).

Entremont was expanded in the mid-third century; it was now separated into Entremont II, Entremont III, and a "lower town" (Figure 5.12) (Benoit 1968, 3). Portions of the ramparts had to be dismantled to accommodate this growth.

Figure 5.13: Picture or rounded street corner at Entremont

Although new fortifications were built, one section of the old wall remained standing in-between Entremont II and III. Both sections demonstrate similar house construction although orientation differs: houses, typically two rows each containing six or seven compartments, were organised back to back and separated by narrow streets 2.5 to 3.5m wide. This grid plan was supplemented by rounded corners at street junctions possibly in order to accommodate traffic (Figure 5.13) (Benoit 1957, 16; 1968, 13; 1975, 233). Most houses in Entremont II were composed of one room 5-8m long by 2.5 to 3.5m wide. Fewer houses contained two or three rooms. Walls were generally fragile and display several phases of rebuilding. This is evidenced by the use of different materials: irregular stone work was adopted and construction in flat rock abandoned (Benoit 1975, 238). Each house contained a dolia, a hearth, and fragments of amphorae, Campanian, and native black-clay Hallstatt pottery.

In the lower town, blocks of houses were twice as large as those in the older section of the settlement. Individual residences can also be distinguished. Units were generally divided into two or three rooms, some of which may have had a second storey. There is some indication that ground floors may have sustained use for production; evidence of weaving, metallurgy, olive presses, glass working, milling, and baking has been uncovered (Goudineau 1984, 119-221; Benoit 1968, 19). Other finds of imported goods, ie amphorae, fine pottery, and Massaliote coins, have also been found (Benoit 1968, 19).

Entremont was destroyed and deserted in 123 BC (Benoit 1975, 230; Harding 2007, 196). The lack of arrentine and samian wares and imperial coins in the settlement indicates that it was not reoccupied during the Roman period. Conversely, other sites in close proximity to Entremont have yielded an abundance of these artefacts (Benoit 1975, 233).

5.5 The changing urban structure

Transalpine Gaul is considered to have been the most Hellenised and, later, the most Romanised region of Gaul. If this were true, then it would follow that any Celtic hillforts in close contact with Mediterranean culture would ultimately develop urban features comparable to those found in archaic states. Although many sites, such as Saint Blaise and Glanum, are of unknown status, it is possible to say that southern Gallic hillforts represent some form of centralised organisation.

Regardless of their status, one thing remains clear: the

nature and development of southern Gallic settlements was different than either the Greek colonies or more northerly Celtic oppida. In central and northern Gaul, oppida could reach 1500ha and were characterised by dispersed houses with no alignment or orientation (Audouze and Büchsenschütz, 1991; Collis 1984; Büchsenschütz 1984; Green 1995, 163). By contrast, southern Gallic sites were limited in size and characterised by classical features such as stone fortifications and rectilinear road networks. They also differed from the Greek colonies: they were situated on hilltops, and lacked "public and monumental architecture prior to the second century BC" (Dietler 1997, 308).

There are certain aspects of urbanism to bear in mind when discussing these last points. Although some demonstrate familiarity and a degree of Hellenic influence, they also demonstrate a lack of understanding or a difference of technique.

The appearance of ramparts in the late seventh and early sixth centuries have been cited as being an indicator of early Massaliote influence.[8] There are two problems with this idea. First, fortification construction may have been enhanced by Classical contact, however, the basic methods of construction were not unknown to the Celto-Ligurians; the earth and timber construction techniques were replaced by various methods involving stone. Secondly, the Hellenic circuit around Massalia was erected at a relatively late date, as is indicated by black-glazed pottery, the latest examples of which barely date before the mid-second century BC (Euzennat 1980, 134-136).

The walls at Saint-Blaise and Glanum which bare resemblance are also of a relatively contemporaneous with the "Wall of Crinas" at Massalia (Tréziny 1985, 145). Similarities in craftsmanship are undeniable: joints "a crochet," herringbone detail, the presence of mason's marks (Benoit 1966, 15-17), and the provision of stone for Saint-Blaise and the "Wall of Crinas" from the quarry at Cap Courrone[9]. But, the ways in which those blocks were prepared and placed differed between all three sites.

At Massalia, the edges of the blocks were bevelled with a double bladed hammer prior to placement. This was to prevent damaging the edges during placement of the stone. The herringbone pattern was the result of the bevelling process and only visible on the lower foundations (Benoit 1966, 17). This technique is known in Greece, most notably at Thaos (Martin 1965, 385, pl. 44 and 2). Conversely, at Saint-Blaise, the blocks were positioned first (Bessac 1980, 143). The edges of the face of the stone were then adorned with the herringbone detail, leaving a border 2-3cm larger (Benoit 1966, 17; Rolland 1951, 91). The detail was made with a sharp tool, which left slightly concave traces, deposited in long lines of chevrons. The size of the herringbone differs from one site to another. Therefore, it is possible to say that both walls adhere to a similar architectural tradition although the technique differs profoundly.[10]

Rolland (1958, 79-80; 1957, 119) and Benoit (1966, 18) think that the fortification at Saint-Blaise was the prototype upon which the constructions at Glanum were based.[11] The fortification wall at Glanum cannot be definitely dated and two different methods of construction were employed in its construction (Rolland 1958, 85-86): the older section of the western wall on the Sacred Way utilises the herringbone detail, while the joint between the older wall and the newer section uses juxtaposed joints. Likewise, several construction techniques were used at Glanum which were not attested at Saint-Blaise. Some of the blocks have holes, suggesting they were lifted into place. The foundations are relatively weak in comparison because the foundation trenches are shallower. Cleaning and dressing of the stones is less homogeneous and some blocks are carved with a narrow border (Rolland 1958, 79-80). Benoit (1966, 18) suggests that these nuances of construction suggest a degeneration of Greek building techniques. The constructions are, therefore, installed to give back some glory to Massalia.

The significance of towers is also problematic. In many cases, the towers were either too few in number or too close together rendering them useless. Even where regularly spaced towers were present they were only common for a short period. For instance, in southern France regularly spaced towers begin to appear in the mid-third century BC, but are rare by the late second century BC. It is interesting to note that tower shape differed between Languedoc and Provence. In Provence, indigenous construction traditions were employed until the fourth century BC, when round and ovoid towers were replaced by Greek-style rectangular ones. The opposite is true of Languedoc. Towers were rectangular until the third century BC. After this point, round construction became preferential (Dietler 1997, 312). The presence of towers and the regional changes in shape are probably representative of indirect influence rather than the result of direct imitation. They are most likely an indigenous response to changing social and economic factors (see chapter 4), or a "recourse to indigenous notions rather than technical reasons" (Tréziny 1992, 337).

Similar problems exist internally. Evidence demonstrating the adoption and/or adaptation of Greek-style urban planning is obvious, ie orthogonal layout, and rectangular, regular insulae. However, differences between typical poleis and the layouts of Celtic oppidum are still noticeable.

---

[8] Conversely, Morel (1995, 46) suggests that Etruscans are actually responsible for introducing rampart building techniques to the indigenous population. He bases this on the early instalment of ramparts and the presence of mud-brick at Saint-Blaise, L'Arquet, Tamaris, and Martigues.
[9] Evidence is provided through literary sources (Strabo 4.1.6), archaeological study (Benoit 1936, 49, no. 156) and through scientific analysis carried out at La Laboratoire de Geologie historique et de Paleontologie de Marseille. For further details see Goudineau 1984, 220.

[10] For a detailed discussion of techniques, methods and tools, see Bessac 1980.
[11] Several of the monumental structures are adorned with herringbone detail. See Rolland 1958. Rolland (1957, 119) even suggests that the military architecture of Saint-Blaise was the inspiration for the monumental architecture of Glanum, i.e the chicane doors, round merlons, and the enclosure of the sanctuary. Other structures, such as the House of Sulla, and the later twin temples erected under Agrippa also attest to a stronger connection with Saint-Blaise than of Marseille.

Subtle variations in the treatment and partitioning of public and private space attest to the underlying persistence of indigenous societal conceptions (see Dedet 1999; Tréziny 1992). Even in the most stringently planned settlements, like Entremont, these indigenous spatial distinctions are apparent. Furthermore, a main component of any classical site is the presence of public buildings and monuments, ie the bouleuterion, agora, or forum and basilica. In many Celtic hilltop settlements, such as Ensérune and Saint Blaise, these buildings are absent. No evidence has been found to indicate they were ever built, and in instances in which they were, as at Glanum, there is no indication that they were used as was meant by classical standards. Furthermore, most sites lack the continuity and the affluence that Glanum enjoyed. Many of the largest oppida, such as Entremont, Ensérune, and Saint Blaise, were destroyed before Transalpine Gaul was annexed by the Romans. Many of the "cities" belonging to later periods do not possess either continuity or their origins in Celtic settlements, but are equipped with public architecture since many were founded or built by the Romans themselves. Therefore, it is not until subsequent periods (Goodman 2007, 83-89; Goudineau 1991; Rivet 1988) that "Hellenisation" or "Romanisation" can be thought to have made a significant and pervasive impact on the indigenous population.

It is important to distinguish what is representative of an actual change in a way of life and what is simply masking the indigenous institutions. This is often hard, if not impossible. Some of the urban development may never have been installed to serve their classical function. They may have only been intended as a form of imitation. For example, the Latin and Greek alphabet was sometimes used to write Celtic languages and names, or to express Celtic beliefs (Nicols 1987; Bats 2004). To the same extent, the agora may have been used to display severed heads and not for civic administrative purposes. Furthermore, differences are apparent even outside of the civic domain.

Chapter 6
Art and Cult Sanctuaries

6.1 Introduction

The Gallic and "Germanic Celts" did seem to possess a willingness to extract forms, elements, and techniques from trade objects initially imported from Massalia (see chapter 4). These cannot be viewed, however, as definitive indicators of the penetration of Greek influence into the internal social structure of a settlement, or on a larger scale, a culture. A better indicator of incorporation and/or adoption of foreign ideas by the indigenous population may be through art, sanctuary architecture, and religion.

Before undertaking a discussion of the religious rites, it is necessary to discuss the changing artistic representations of the Celtic World. Two different types of art arose: the La Tène style, which was confined to northern and central Gaul, and the southern Gallic Celtic art forms.

6.2 La Tène

The La Tène style is thought to have first developed in the middle Rhineland (Wells 1984, 141; Megaw 1970, 276; Driehaus 1966; Schaaff 1969) between c. 550 to 500 BC. The culture quickly spread and became prominent throughout the regions spanning eastern France and Bohemia. Included in this area were the mid-Rhenish regions associated with the chieftain burials, the east and north-east of France responsible for the chariot burials, eastern Bavaria, western Bohemia, and southern Thuringia (De Navarro 1928, 424-425). Despite the varying settlement patterns present across this area (see above), Celtic artistic interpretation and incorporation of Mediterranean style can be found. For instance, examples have been discovered in the burials of Kleinaspergle (see above), Hunsrück-Eifel, Rhine-Mosel (Driehaus 1966), Rhine-Saar (Schaaff 1969), and throughout the Marne Valley. Most of these early La Tène artefacts uncovered in these regions display variations of several Classical themes: upper triple leafed half palmettes, double lobes with associated double circles, and simplified lotus buds (Megaw 1972, 277). These forms were replicated using punch or beaded edging - techniques which produce effects similar to those used to decorate the couch of Hochdorf.

These are specific examples however. The La Tène style can be generally characterised by the fusion of older bronze and iron age technical and stylistic elements with new Mediterranean influences (De Navarro 1928, 424). It can be further distinguished from earlier Hallstatt traditions by its curvilinear forms; rectilinear and/or geometric motifs were no longer employed and schematic representations of humans were abandoned for more stylised circular forms (see Figure 3.11). Even more stylised was the Celtic art of metal-working. While this too has evidence of Mediterranean influence, characteristically Celtic elements are more prominent. Following phases of La Tène art became much more abstract and blended more with local Celtic bronze and iron age influences. This resulted in the production of art in which it is much more difficult to distinguish Classical elements from those of Celtic origin. It has been suggested by De Navarro (1928, 427) that this can be attributed to the decrease in Mediterranean imports during La Tène B.

The fact that Massalia provided the primary influence during the late Hallstatt and early La Tène periods is often used to support the view that much of Europe north of the Alps was peripheral and subject to the conquering cultures of the Mediterranean. Yet, the art produced during this time indicates this idea is erroneous; the regional art continues to develop and spread long after northern Gaul and Germany ceased importing Mediterranean goods as explained above. While classical art is narrative, Celtic art is not and is produced in small scale (Green 1989, 206). There is an occasional representation of foreign subject matter, ie dancing, weaving, and burial rites, which are mostly confined to funerary pottery or metalwork of the Hallstatt period. For the most part, little to no continuity exists in the transition from Hallstatt D to early La Tène culture (Megaw and Megaw 1995, 354).

As mentioned above, a wealth of factors contributed to the segregation of northern and central Gaul from Massalia including changing trade routes, the abandonment of princely sites, and the rise of new groups of settlements in the Hunsrück-Eifel and Marne regions. As a result, the La Tène culture did not spread below the river Durance or into southern Gaul for two centuries (Benoit 1975, 226). During this time, it becomes clear that while the rest of Gaul began to demonstrate "ornamental inorganic decoration of utilitarian objects" (Bober 1948, 411), southern Gaul developed its own indigenous artistic style (described in detail below). This is most prominently displayed in the cult sites of Entrement, Ensérune, and Roquepertuse, although statues have also been found at Glanum and Saint Blaise. Through the analysis of the sanctuary architecture, associated statuary, and artwork, it may be possible to

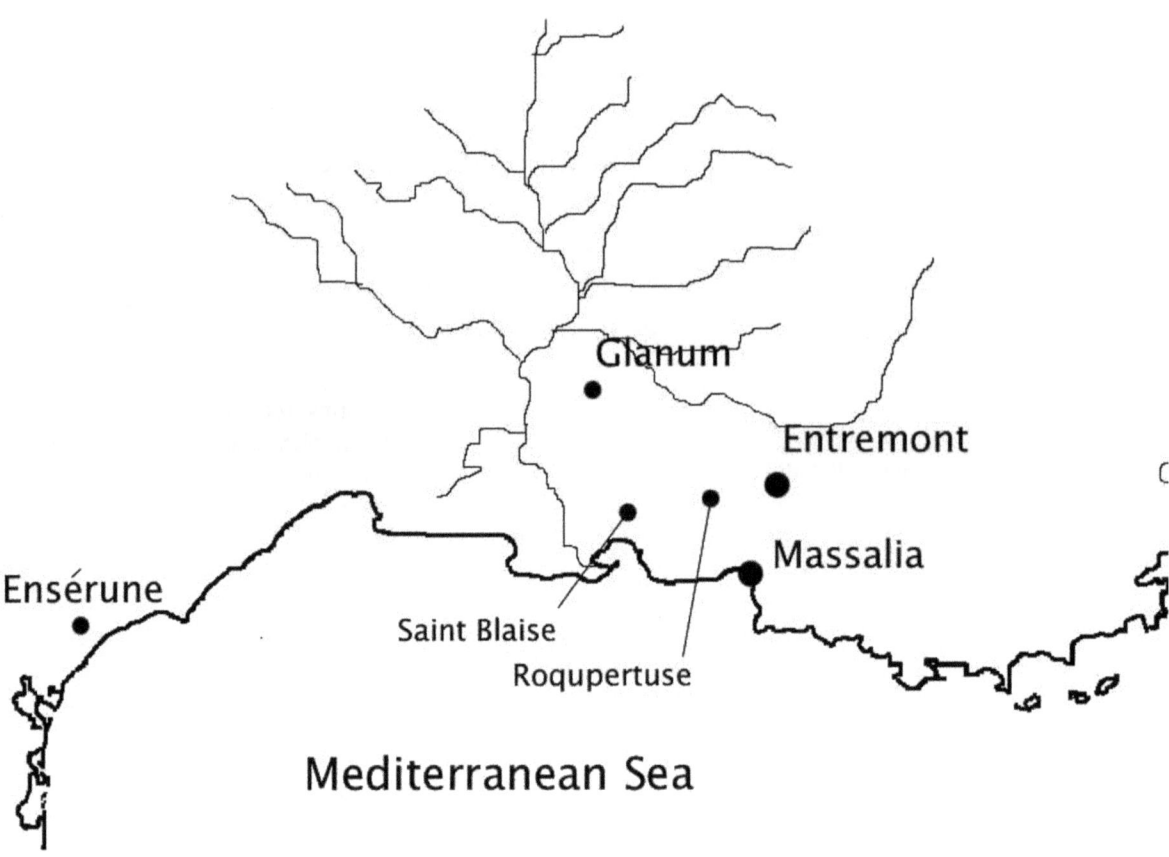

Figure 6.1: Distribution map of discussed indigenous sanctuaries in Southern Gaul

determine the extent to which Mediterranean ways of life were adopted by the indigenous population.

6.3 Cult sites and sanctuaries

Cult sites in southern France (Figure 6.1) pre-date the official Roman annexation of Transalpine Gaul, although the symbiotic relationship between Rome and Massalia had allowed the Romans to be involved in the area long before it was absorbed into the Empire. Most of these settlements were founded before the third century BC. As discussed previously, they were initially Celto-Ligurian sanctuaries and cannot easily be reconstructed through excavation and analysis of the artefacts. However, certain sites, such as Roquepertuse and Glanum, have lead to the conclusion that they were centred upon ritual focus.

6.3.1 Entremont

It is clear that the sanctuary at Entremont went through several phases. Unfortunately, the location of the oldest phase, Entremont I, cannot be reconciled due to the modern military occupation of the site. But, there are indications that such a phase existed: several aniconic stelae (see chapter five on Urbanism), are re-used in the fourth/third century ramparts and as flooring in the last phase of the shrine (Benoit 1975, 245). As mentioned above, the final phase of the sanctuary was a colonnaded building located between two rampart towers at one end of the Sacred Way (Harding 2007, 199; Benoit 1975, 246).

The sanctuary ("the Sanctuary of Skulls"), and the associated internal shrine, are one storey high and have paved floors (Benoit 1957, 28). Although not fully excavated, the site has yielded numerous finds: statues, carvings, and human remains, mostly consisting of crushed skulls belonging to men between twenty and fifty years of age. No cervical vertebrae were found and several skulls demonstrate evidence of mummification and/or have puncture marks, attesting to ritual use (Benoit 1969, 21).

The portico of the shrine is comprised of seven quadrangular pillars belonging to two separate phases. The first phase included four pillars each measuring 0.35-0.45m wide. Of the four pillars, three were re-used and incorporated into the hypostyle room in the "Sanctuary of Skulls," while the fourth was re-used in the east tower of the rampart. Each pillar was carved: one with niches utilised to display human skulls and one with reliefs of serpents. The third (Figure 6.2a), 2.60m in length, was carved with twelve mouthless severed heads (têtes coupées), the last of which is upside down (Benoit 1975, 245). A lintel (Figure 6.2b), also re-used in the sanctuary, is thought to have been contemporary with these pillars. It is engraved with a mouthless severed head and associated skull niches (Benoit 1969, 20).

The second phase is composed of three quadrangular pillars, each measuring 0.40m wide. Three sides of each pillar are carved with horsemen carrying lances. In one scene, a horseman has a severed head hanging from the horses' withers, in front of which a nude figure pays homage to a tomb decorated with several têtes coupées, all of whom

Art and Cult Sanctuaries

Figure 6.2: (A) Pillar with twelve mouthless heads (Hodge 1998, 210, fig. 127). (B) Lintel with depiction of a head and two skull niches (Drawing L. Laing)

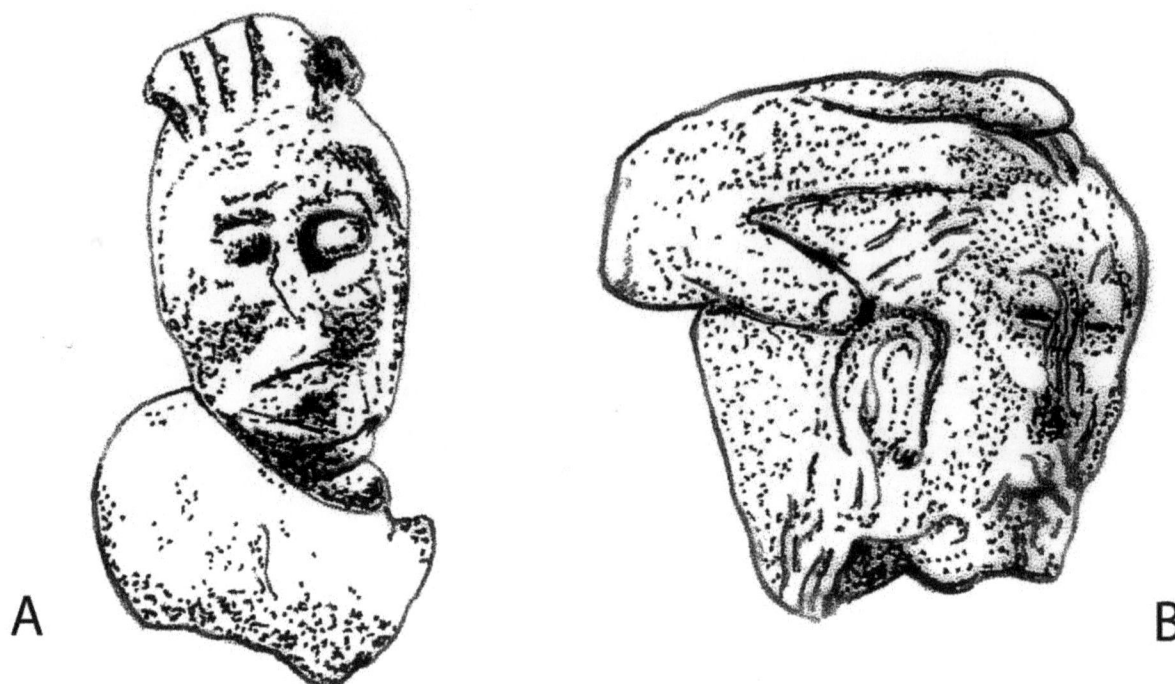

Figure 6.3: Severed heads with hands (Drawing L. Laing)

have closed eyes. Such rituals are described by Diodorus (V, 29) and Strabo (IV, 4,5):

"The Celts, they say, attach the decapitated head of the enemy's leader at the withers of their mount; they nail these lugubrious trophies to the door of their house and embalm the heads of the most illustrious enemies..."

The clothing and the weapons depicted suggest a contemporary date with the Celto-Ligurian occupation of the site.

The approach to the sanctuary along the Sacred Way has also yielded several artefacts, among which are crushed cranial bone and fragments of statues. The skull fragments are not contemporary with those found inside the sanctuary. They probably date to the period following the destruction of the site, as indicated by a catapult ball found in the fill (Benoit 1975, 246). Of the statue fragments recovered, the most interesting depicts a human hand clutching a severed head (the significance is described below) (Figure 6.3). Each head has closed eyes, downturned mouth, and in one case, the ears are back to front. Other fragmentary evidence includes single and grouped heads, some of which wear leather helmets, and a torso which seems to be wearing a torc (Harding 2007, 199).

6.3.2 Roquepertuse

Roquepertuse is located in the Arc valley, approximately one kilometre from Velaux. Upon study, it becomes evident that it was never an important settlement (Gérin-Ricard 1927, 38). Instead, the site gained prestige as a sanctuary (Clerc 1916, 103, 110) and went through several stages: ancient sacred space, open air sanctuary, and finally, the terraced sanctuary dating between the sixth and second century BC. During the second century, Roquepertuse was destroyed by the Romans (Gérin-Ricard 1927, 41).

The sanctuary was accessed by a staircase, composed of five steps measuring 1.42 metres each (Gérin-Ricard 1927, 14). These lead to two superimposed platforms. The earliest platform was polygonal with four sides of different length - 2.5m, 3.5m, 5m, and 7m. This was later replaced by a trapezoidal terrace (Gérin-Ricard 1927, 14) surrounded by two walls: the first wall was 3.5m long, while the second measured 2.8m long.

In its final phase of the sanctuary was furnished with a portico consisting of painted quadrangular pillars with skull niches, lintels carved with horses and/or têtes coupées, and a sculpture of a goose (Benoit 1965, 19; Harding 2007, 196, 199). Other statues included double heads carved from local limestone and cross-legged statues (accroupis) similar to those found in Entremont (Benoit 1965, 42; Benoit 1975, 256). Accroupis from both sites have evidence of vermillion and carmine coloured paint (Benoit 1965, 42; Barbet 1991). Because there are no associations enabling more precise dating, the statues could have been carved at any point during the fourth to the second centuries BC.

6.3.3 Glanum

While Glanum (described above) is not representative of the general urban development of southern Gaul, the settlement presents an interesting dichotomy. Despite the presence of Classical public architecture, Glanum still possesses Celtic characteristics similar to other indigenous hilltop sites (Arcelin 1990). It was probably initially founded as a sanctuary; the landscape is terraced and the rampart seems to have been built only to protect the sanctuary. Since the site also has a comparatively prolonged continuity, the discussion will again be curtailed, beginning at the sixth century and ending at the second century BC.

It is hard to discuss Glanum without reference to the wealth of different religious architecture. As a result, it is necessary to discuss in which way it is best to understand its development during the Hellenic period. There are two main ways: individually consider each building, or analyze Glanum as a sum of its components.

If each building is considered individually, it is easier to define Glanum as an urban settlement consisting of several cult sanctuaries and monumental public buildings. Examining buildings as isolated features would be problematic in terms of trying to interpret the settlement as a whole; it would neglect any attempt of understanding the social relations present. The development of Glanum may have been religiously-driven, as was observed in Britain during the second century AD with the construction of the healing spa at Springhead (Andrews 2007, 31-36). Public buildings would have, therefore, all had a religious purpose: the landscape would thus be divided into different centres of religious activity. Haeussler (2007, 87) suggests, that different "levels of initiation" would be present "within the triangle formed by the sacred spring (via sacra), rock sanctuary, and Tuscan temple" (see Figure 5.10). Glanum would then serve not only the religious activities of the local population, but would also have been transformed into a Salluvian political-religious centre. This may have been the reason for its destruction in 125 BC. Furthermore, Haeussler (2007, 88) also suggests that the Greek religious iconography, incorporated into the second century architectural repertoire, was utilised alongside Celtic deities, to help "define a position in a world that was dominated by Greek culture and Roman power."

6.4 Religion

Analysis and examination of the architecture and art can provide information regarding the changing social and ideological structure of Celtic communities during the transition from Hallstatt to La Tène. This is especially true of the period spanning the sixth to first centuries BC: during this time the "complex process of conurbanisation in Europe," took place (Jope 1995, 376). What becomes problematic is attempting to reconstruct iron age religious beliefs and cult rituals. This is due to both the lack of epigraphic evidence and the nature of the literary material available. In order to make any type of inference on religious belief systems, we would have to rely on available classical sources. One must use caution when referencing literary sources since ancient writers often present a view of events as a descriptive comparison to their own societies. An applicable example is seen in Lucan's Pharsalia (III, 412-417):

> "...*simulacraque maesta deorum*
> *Arte carent caesique extant informia truncis.*
> *Ipse situs putrique facit iam robore pallor*
> *Attonitos; non vulgatis sacrata figures*
> *Numina sic metuunt: tantum terroribus addit,*
> *Quos timeant, non nosse deos"*[1]

It is useful to review primary evidence that relates religious activity, beliefs, and iconography to the Celts themselves. Thus, Celtic art provides the most direct way to distinguish between "classicisation" of religious beliefs and "classicisation" of purely Celtic artistic constructs. As Megaw and Megaw (1995, 355-366) state, Celtic art is a "visible expression of a system of ideas, where even the most seemingly non-representational motifs may have a precise, perhaps, religious meaning...The archaeological record suggests as much regional diversity in belief systems as in more tangible categories of material culture." Therefore, symbolic traits in visual art which are identifiable on both a regional and chronological scale may indicate the selective incorporation of ideas that are widely applicable to varying regional belief systems (Megaw and Megaw 1995, 366). It is important to remember, however, that attestations of specific beliefs (ie defixiones, or curse tablets) are rare. Shrines, associated objects, and art can only provide a suggestion of the rituals observed.

It is impossible to reconstruct religious practices and belief systems. The archaeological evidence, however, may allow for an association between form and belief. The social importance of artistic compositional changes is ultimately clear when considering the amount of labour needed to construct a cultic shrine, comparable only to the efforts made in fortifying a hillfort. The creation of new cult places and statues are therefore the result of a long-term process by which new pantheons are developed, with associated changes in myth and practice (Haeussler 2007, 82-84). While this very well might be true, there is no substantive evidence to suggest that old ideals were either combined with, or abandoned for, new Mediterranean ones. Archaeological material does indicate however, a uniformity of artistic creations incorporating the areas of the Pyrenees, Loire, Seine, and the Marne Valley (Pobé and Roubier 1961, 13). The Celtic patterns and traditional symbols remain fundamentally unaltered, even though the appearance is adjusted in response to Mediterranean contact (Green 1989, 206).

In light of the evidentiary material, it is clear that there needs to be a differentiation between artistic presentation and Classicisation. Consequently, we must turn our attention to a discussion of the religious statuary found within the aforementioned cult sanctuaries. It is important to point out that identifying indigenous religious architecture is not an easy process. For example, the sanctuaries detailed above were identified by the presence of porticoes, making these structures distinguishable from other buildings because of their size (Garcia 2004, 116; Arcelin et al 1992). Furthermore, in many instances, these religious buildings were situated in-between rows of houses or rampart towers. They were not in a prominent place either in the centre of

---

[1] "the images were stark, gloomy blocks of unworked timber, rotten with age, whose ghastly pallor terrified their devotees – quite another matter from our own rustic statues which are too familiar to cause alarm"

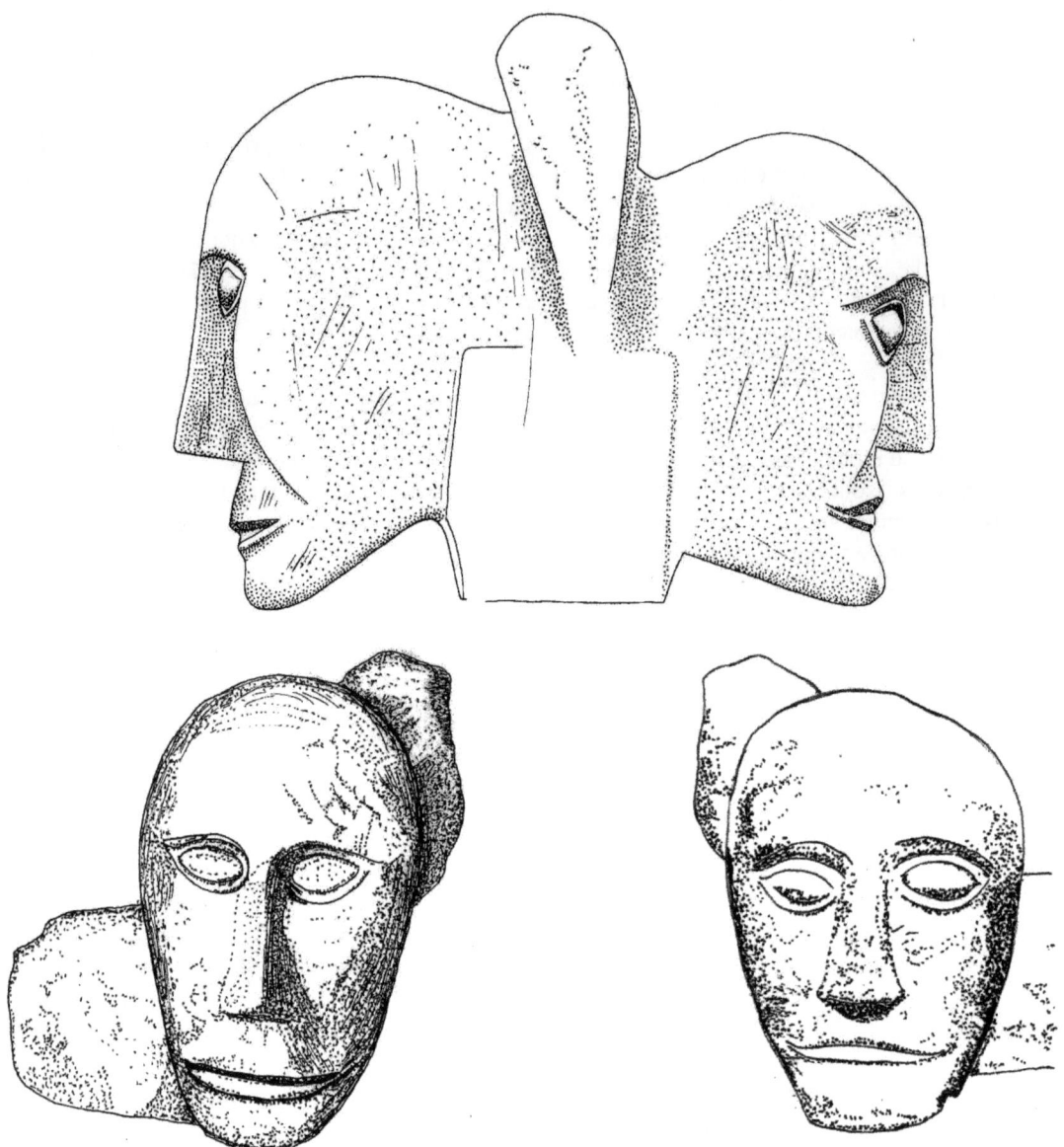

Figure 6.4: (A) Double head of Roquepertuse (Harding 2007, 198, fig. 9.4, 1). (B) Frontal view of head A. (C) Frontal view of head B (Drawings L. Laing)

the city, or as a removed place of worship. As a result, it is difficult to quantify the socio-religious aspects of the community, and, in some cases, identify the religious function at all (Haeussler 2007, 85). In other cases, such as Nîmes and Glanum, the colonnaded buildings were only identified as having cult importance by the find of accroupis. In fewer instances, ie Pech Maho, cult sculpture was associated with burials (Gailledrat and Marchand 2003, 235).

6.4.1 Representation of Celtic cults

It is important to make a distinction between style and meaning of the expressed ideas. Although Celtic religious art may have taken a more Classical form, the beliefs presented by the art, ie those underlying the artistic representation, are no more indicative of Greek than of iron age culture (Green 1989, 6). Instead, they seem to represent an amalgam. Intense processes of social evolution began and were advanced by the complex interaction between two very different social and cultural groups. The Greeks and Romans introduced new factors to the Celtic world by means of education and socio-political ambition. These might not have fundamentally changed indigenous religious beliefs, but definitely altered the artistic methods in which they were transferred. Gallia Narbonensis provides a wealth of archaeological evidence for the formative period which saw the shift of power from the Greeks to the Romans (which is confined to the late La Tène period and early Principate: second century BC – first century AD). Prior to this period, the "classicisation" of southern Gaul allowed the Celts the opportunity to make local beliefs more visually prominent. During this Gallo-Greek syncretism, indigenous identity can be readily seen in the art.

While Celtic art begins to demonstrate a familiarity and proficiency in the use of plastic form (Pobé and Roubier 1961, 16), several typical Celtic characteristics are retained.

Art and Cult Sanctuaries

Figure 6.5: Accroupis statue from Glanum

Figure 6.6: Reconstruction of an accroupis and severed heads (Hodge 1998, 213, fig. 129)

If the double heads of Roquepertuse (Figure 6.4a) are examined, it becomes quite clear that plastic form has been used to more realistically represent the human head. Viewed from the front, the cheeks possess a definite curve and the nose demonstrates identification of attributes such as alae and concavity. The eyes, lentoid and double outlined, the linear representation of the mouth, and the triangular nose (Figure 6.4b), on the other hand, signifies the Celtic artistic typology which has not been abandoned in lieu of greater realism. Even when looked at in profile, the plastic construction of the head loses definition and retreats to the former Celtic methodology: at the end of the cheek bone the cheek rapidly descends into a flat plane. This is more prominent in profiles of Head B (Figure 6.4c) where the cheek does not seem to have been produced with three-dimensional intent at all (Jacobsthal 1944, 4).

The facial realism of these heads is not the first and only display of Classical components. The squatting men sculptures (Figure 6.5), or accroupis, found at Glanum, Roquepertuse, and Entremont, also display both Classical and Celtic components, probably even more prominently than do the double heads of Roquepertuse (Jacobsthal 1944, 6). Similar sculptures have been found from other parts of Gallic lands, such as Beuvray. All seem to be distinguishable from divinities usually associated with cross-legged posture (ie Cernunnos) in style, form, and dress. Due to these characteristics, Haeussler (2007, 84) suggests that perhaps the cross-legged figures are actually "representations of ancestors or heroic figures which acquired divine honour and are thus custodians of the community".[2] A "heroic founder" is a Mediterranean concept which is demonstrated in various stories including the Aenid (Virgil) and by the worship of Greek hero cults (Kearns 1989). Still, caution must be taken so as not to become trapped in suppositional answers to questions that will never have a true response. It is possible to say that the accroupis are of strictly Celtic origin as can be determined by the cross-legged position, patterns of garments, and the presence of torcs. The form of the legs, familiarity with plastic form, presence of the acoteria, and the three-dimensional style, however, is demonstrative of the intensive Greek training of the sculptor. Although some accroupis, such as those from Roquepertuse, lack heads, confining examination of Greek influence primarily to figure and dress, theses sculptures have been of particular interest to scholars. One hand is usually thought to have rested atop severed head (Figure

---

[2] Similarly, Francois Salviat (1987) suggest the statues represent local aristocracy or tribal chieftains. For other discussions see: Lescure 1991; Ducepée-Lamarre 2002.

Culture Contact in Southern Mediterranean France

Figure 6.7: Inscised heads from Entremont showing full progression from linear representation typical of the Celtic artistic style, to a realistic illustration of human heads and facial features (Drawing L. Laing)

6.6) which was positioned on the knee as implicated by evidence found at Entremont, Roquepertuse, and Glanum (see Figure 6.3). Regrettably, no hand-held severed heads have been found still attached to the accroupis statues.[3]

One accroupis from Roquepertuse has lead to the belief that one hand may have held a thunderbolt of Jupiter Taranis: embedded in the stone hand was a small piece of iron (Pobé and Roubier 1961, 15, pl. 32; Benoit 1975, 257, fig. 81; Benoit 1955, pl. XXXIX). If this was true, this would be the first materialisation of a symbolic Mediterranean component. Similarly, it would be possible to suggest that some Mediterranean beliefs were actually being adopted by the indigenous population. But, there is no evidence supporting this reconstruction.

6.5 Summary

The changes in iconographic and religious art was a constant and on-going process in the Celtic, Graeco-Celtic, and Graeco-Roman world. Changes in power had a profound effect upon the areas of Celto-Ligurian oppida (Green 1989, 6). It has been assumed, and somewhat taken for granted, that southern Gaul was not only very Hellenised, but also "well-integrated into the empire-wide social networks" (Haeussler 2007, 83). Yet, while this may become truer in the later Empire, during the mid-Greek and early Principate, a clear line must be drawn between "Hellenisation" or "Romanisation" and religious activity. Based on the archaeological remains, what is altered are not the religious beliefs, but the method, composition, and the means by which ideas are transmitted. This is best demonstrated by the persistence of the Head Cult which does not disappear after several centuries of contact, but only alter its form: the series of incised heads at Entremont (Figure 6.7) range from a suggestive T-shaped face to a full rendition of facial features in the round (Pobé and Roubier 1961, 13-14), the association of accroupis and severed heads, and the double heads of Roquepertuse. All of these examples retain their Celtic meaning and some traits typical of ethnic art, but sacrifice the characterised exaggeration for more classic realism.

These artistic representations make it very easy to define Celtic art in terms of what was borrowed from external influences, and not upon its own inherent artistic merit (Megaw and Megaw 1995, 347). Prior to the infiltration of Mediterranean ways, Celtic art was aniconic and atectonic. Indeed, its evolution owes a lot to the Mediterranean cultures from which it developed certain traditions. In some ways, it is also true that Celtic religious art is anything but purely Celtic (Green 1989, 23-26). This should not lead to the belief that art of the Celtic world was artificially produced by mimicking the traditions of other peoples and cultures. It is merely the product of outside influences providing a new form in which indigenous ideals are transferred. Despite the overarching external influences, it is evident in the art of Gaul that "Celticity" has a subtle, yet pervasive simultaneous influence (Jope 1995, 377, 395). Similarly, they also possibly allow for the ethnicity of the artisan or craftsman to be determined through the various details provided within the style and form of the sculpture, votive, or metalwork. Examples include the un-Greek mouths of the third century Roquepertuse heads and, in general, the highly-developed Celto-Ligurian characterisation of their own ethnic type. This has lead to the conclusion that these were produced by a Classically trained Gaul.

The indigenous Gallic cults did persist, albeit disguised by Mediterranean artistic influence. The worship of Celtic deities persisted, but in Latin forms: the use of epigraphy and theonyms, and later through the use of Roman votive objects and sculpture (Haeussler 2007, 82). What becomes relevant for examination and future research is that none of these aspects of Celtic religious art seem to persist after the early Principate (second century). As stated above, the most diagnostic evidence for the continuity of sites – both settlement and religious contexts – comes from settlements which were destroyed and abandoned with the advent of the Romans. However, even in Glanum the Greek mythological capitals, the indigenous statuary of accroupis, and later, the altar in the bouleuterion, were buried (Haeussler 2007, 88-89). In essence, they were not buried as sacred objects, but as construction waste. The altar, for instance, was used as fill to raise the floor level (CAG 13/2, no. 100, p. 322, 56). This makes it very difficult to say whether or not the associated Celtic ideals live on (either as is or in modified form) into the Roman Period (Haeussler 2007, 83).

---

[3] Likewise, not all *accroupis* may have been sculpted with heads resting on the knee.

Chapter 7
Overview of Gallic Relations with the Greek World

Southern Gaul was thought to have been the most Hellenised region and fully incorporated into the Greek world. Several aspects – trade, burial, urbanism, art, and religion – were explored in order to quantify this process of acculturation. Before concluding, it is necessary to consider certain problems concerning a number of aspects of this study not previously discussed. These are mainly concerned with trade and urbanism.

7.1 Early Massaliote and Phocaean influence: trade and burial

Although Massalia was founded in the sixth century BC, by the Classical Period it comprised of a disparate group of Phocaeans: the mother city had been destroyed and Massalia was left to forge relationships of its own. As a result, close economic and social ties with the indigenous population were formed (Herodotus 1.163-5; Thucydides 1.13.6; Plutarch Solon 2.7; Athenaios 13.36.2-17; Justin 43.3.4-5.10; Aulus Gellius Noctes Atticae 10.16.4.2; Livy 5.34.8; Pomponius Mela 2.77.3-4; Pliny the Elder Natural History 3.34.6-35.1; Strabo 3.4.6-8; 4.1.4; 14.2.10). Despite the numerous literary sources and associated archaeological evidence, the Phocaean and/or Massaliote role in the transmission of Mediterranean goods and ideas remains uncertain. This is further complicated by the presence of pre-colonial (dating prior to the foundation of Massalia) artefacts. In order to clarify these issues, two questions need to be answered: how did the trade networks operate? and to what extent were the Greeks the predominate suppliers of these goods? Traditional trade models led to the assumption that the Greeks played a dual role, being both suppliers and importers. However, distribution patterns of amphorae and various other Mediterranean wares have indicated that these models may not be correct.

While goods were transported far up the Rhône and Seine, the greatest density of imports and Massaliote colonies was along the coast and around the Rhône. This became ever truer after the spread of the La Tène culture separated southern Gaul from the northern and central regions. In the sixth and fifth centuries BC, locally-produced Massaliote pottery, Greek sympotic pottery, and amphorae were traded through southern Gaul (Lomas 2006, 181). This distribution suggests that the strongest links between Massalia and the indigenous population lay in the immediate hinterland of the Greek colony. The distribution of Greek luxury goods farther up the Rhône at sites such as Vix, Seurre, and Châtillon-sur-Glâne, have been cited as an indication that the local population took an active role in the mechanisms of exchange. If this was true, than the pattern of distribution would suggest that trade was aimed at élite indigenous populations gathered in centralised settlements (ie hillforts) who took an interest in the importation of foreign luxury goods (Dietler 1989; Bats 1998, 624-630; Morel 1990, 277-292; Shefton 1989). However, there is no indication that any of the large sites situated in central or northern Gaul acted as distribution centres or took an active interest in the transmission of foreign goods.

Regardless of any existing regional differences in indigenous social systems, the Phocaeans were not the only source of Greek or Mediterranean wares. This is true of both the pre-colonial and the colonial periods in Gaul. Unfortunately, though much discussion has been generated by the archaeological evidence, especially the pre-colonial finds, it remains difficult to identify the agents responsible for their transportation and trade. The Etruscans had also established overland routes to the Danube, river routes along the Po, and founded the port cities of Adria and Spina. Similarly, Rhodian influence is attested by both ancient literary sources as well as archaeological ones.

Further research must be done in order to assess whether there was an economic domination of one distributing group over another, and to better quantify trade routes and the mechanisms by which trade was initiated and operated. In recent years, there has been much study centred on the chemical analysis of amphorae assemblages found at major sites such as Höhenasperg, the Heuneberg, Châtillon-sur-Glâne, and Massalia. The focus of these studies is two-fold: to identify where the amphorae were produced and what they were used to transport. Unfortunately, much of this research is still unpublished and inaccessible.

7.2 Problems of assessing Hellenic influence on urban structure

In attempting to identify and study the process of urbanisation in southern Gaul, several problems are evident. First, very few sites have survived, either completely or partially, to the present day. The ones that do, only do so because of a change in the location of the primary settlement, changes during the middle ages, or abandonment sparred the site subsequent building phases and modern settlement. Nonetheless, many have been altered either by continuous development and occupation, or damaged by ploughing and farming. In these cases, it is important to remember that history is based upon more than the surviving fragments of standing architecture or any accompanying epigraphic evidence. Second, residential areas are seldom subjected to full excavation. Exceptions exist in very few instances, such as Glanum (discussed above) and Vaison. Similarly, southern France has lacked both the systematic, coherent surveys of settlements as well as full publications of finds - a problem which has only recently begun to be remedied. Third, a preoccupation with small-finds and material objects, such as pottery, metal, and stone tools, has hindered the examination of the process of urbanisation as a whole. Likewise, the changes in the internal structure and order of settlements, as well as the accompanying social evolution, have been left without thorough study.

A more serious dilemma exists: the most extensive and detailed information derives from settlements which did not survive the late third and second century BC Roman involvement. Many questions concerning the continuity of beliefs, trade, and politico-economic relationships are consequently left unanswered. As a result, the view and knowledge of the region remains incomplete. Until thorough excavation and study of towns with continuous occupation to and beyond the Roman Period is undertaken, the understanding of the development of southern Gaul remains difficult to reconstruct. On-going research on Massaliote economic-history through the study of pottery (Villard, 1960; Maggetti and Schwab 1982), Hellenic influence in Gaul, and the territory subject to Massalia provides new insights. Without the full publication and systematic excavation of sites, it is nearly impossible to reconstruct the history of the region.

Particular questions may never be answered, at least with any degree of certainty. For instance, when the identification of the initial stages of a site is possible, it is important to ask: What was the status of the site and how did it develop? Did it become an important site? What was the relationship with Massalia initially and how did it progress? As Février (1973, 12) states, "to be able to recognise a settlement is different from attempting to determine its relative importance from either its geographic position or identify its political, economic, or social function." For example, for decades sites in southern Gaul were determined to be entrepôts or emporia based on the Attic, Greek, and Italian pottery found (Février 1973, 12). However, as explained above, the concern with these material objects often clouds our chances of understanding the bigger picture. Greek ceramics at a particular site demonstrates trade but does not prove it was a centre of redistribution. It is important, not to disregard this material evidence, but use it in conjunction with architectural and other finds to reconstruct the way of life, the level of material culture, technological advancements, and possibly even the relationship held with the outside world. Hellenistic ramparts and any changes in the internal settlement patterns, ie grids and regular houses, should begin a debate as to whether this is urbanisation or just a matter of settlement evolution. Are the ramparts an indicator of influence or did Massaliote craftsmen personally help construct the fortifications? If so, did Massalia have political power over this site? The last question is unanswerable.

7.2.1 The ordering of settlements: planning

Before summarising any conclusions, it is crucial to comment on certain aspects of urbanisation that have either been assumed or misinterpreted. Paramount among the problems mentioned above is the automatic assumption that the replacement of a dispersed settlement by an organised layout is representative of a change in social relations. This is not necessarily true. Either fortunately or unfortunately, this change in settlement pattern is easily recognised by archaeologists: it is a feature that has long been attached to a certain conception of ordered society and its associated social relationships. It remains true that all settlements are arranged around a "coherent structural organisation that is integral to the connection between the structuring of social relations and daily practice" (Dietler 1997, 310-311). This pertains even to the dispersed and "unorganised" settlements typical in southern Gaul during the first few decades of the fifth century BC. The social relationships responsible for these particular settlement arrangements, however, are not always easily identifiable or quantifiable. This is mainly because it is not always possible to reconstruct the sociology of the culture which produced them in the first place (Dietler and Herbich 1993; Dietler and Herbich 1998; Fernandez 1977; Herbich and Dietler 1993; Rapoport 1969). The substitution of a "haphazard" settlement arrangement for a planned one is, therefore, not necessarily suggestive of a change in social relations but more representative of outside influence.

7.3 Hellenic influence?

With this in mind, it cannot be said that southern Gaul was untouched by Greek influence. Although potentially misleading, the most obvious indicator is the evidence of a planned settlement. For example, the corners of buildings located on street junctions at Entremont are rounded to accommodate traffic. It must be remembered that the nature and development of these settlements is different from both the Greek colonies and Celtic oppida in more northerly regions (explained above).

The level of Hellenic influence present in these settlements was little more than a thin veneer: the towers incorporated into the circuit defences were too close to have been functional, public and private space were treated differently, and public buildings were absent. The latter of these examples is perhaps the most telling. In both Greek and Roman urban settings, many daily activities and social relationships were centred on public buildings such as an agora or basilica. Even when present, as at Glanum, there is no way to demonstrate that public architecture was used the same way as in the classical city. Glanum's unusual development and ostensible wealth is probably attributable to its position on several main trade routes and its ability to cater for various religions; itinerant workers or merchants, with different ideological concepts, would have travelled those routes making their way to the next market. Even if one were to ignore later developments and Glanum's continuity, the initial development was probably focused around the spring, sustaining use as a religious sanctuary and explaining many of its attributes.

7.3.1 Celtic Influence in Massalia

Cultural interaction works both ways. Finds within Marseille suggest either a Celtic presence within the city of the use of Celtic products by the Greek settlers. A house located in Saint-Laurent (a quarter of Marseille) dates to the first quarter of the sixth century and was built of mud-brick and stone. It presented a pottery assemblage comprising eighteen to twenty per cent indigenous ceramics (Gantès 1992a, 75). Two contemporary houses and located two hundred metres away from the first house, were built in indigenous fashion using a timber frame (Gantès1992a, 72-75; Morel 1995, 47).

Literary sources also attest to the to Massaliote relations with the surrounding indigenous population. For instance, St. Jerome (In Galat. 2.426, p. 543) and Isidore of Seville (15.1.63) records that Varro stated that the Massaliotes were tri-lingual, speaking Greek, Latin and Gallic.[1]

These archaeological remains present an interesting picture as well as a problem which is difficult to solve. As mentioned above, ancient Massalia is, at times, difficult to reconstruct because of its continuous occupation. As a result, the archaeological remains become increasingly important in resolving this issue. Indigenous finds are rare but can be misconstrued. While one of the houses mentioned above is built in indigenous fashion, the area in which it was found seems to have used stone, mud-brick, and timber in domestic architecture between 600 and 580 BC (Gantès 1992a, 72). Likewise, in chapter four it was demonstrated that Massalia became increasingly dependent on the surrounding Celtic settlements for the production and provision of certain ceramics, some of which are "Mediterranean" in inspiration[2]. Some of this production began almost immediately after Massaliote production. Certain pottery types, such as grey-monochrome wares, contained a high percentage of indigenous forms even though they were of foreign manufacture. Conversely, indigenous pottery traditions began to incorporate Mediterranean designs and/or imitate them. It is, therefore, not surprising that the early assemblages from the house in Saint-Laurent contained a high percentage of indigenous forms. This is particularly true of indigenous non-turned pottery which comprised between eight to fifteen per cent of the total ceramics found in Marseille during the first half century of its foundation (Gantès 1992b, 176).

Consequently, it is also unsurprising that Massalia was tri-lignual. The establishment of such an early economic inter-dependence would have been better facilitated by a mutual knowledge of Greek, Latin and/or Gallic.

---

[1] For a more in-depth discussion of the literary sources, see Momigliano 1976.
[2] See pages 37-40.

7.4 Conclusion

Although this study has attempted to analyze the gradual "acculturation" of the Celtic peoples in southern Gaul, there is one over-arching problem that makes any kind of conclusion difficult. A culture is manifested when "a group or society of people expresses its ideas in the manufacture of objects, the construction of buildings and the organisation of the landscape, while, conversely, with each action resulting in one of these products, it re-creates these ideas" (Derks 1998, 18-19). First, it has already been stated that the development of a planned settlement is not necessarily indicative of a change in social relations. All settlements, disperse and un-oriented or not, are arranged according to the social relationships present in the society. Whether or not these relationships can be identified or quantified is not always a matter readily resolved. Second, it must be remembered that the Mediterranean goods found at Höhenasperg, Hohmichele, Vix, and the Heuneberg, have value because they are exotic. While their presence indicates a sort of supply-and-demand, no evidence has been uncovered to suggest that these settlements took part in any system redistributing foreign items. Even when the distribution of Mediterranean goods is widespread, as is the case with bucchero and Attic wares, there is no definitive answer as to whether or not luxury items were used in daily activities or only for ritualistic use. Amphorae, on the other hand, may indicate incorporation of Mediterranean foods and liquids, such as wine, oil, and pastes, into the Celtic diet. However, conclusions are only tentative until residue analysis becomes available. Therefore, Mediterranean goods found in Celtic settlements in northern and central Gaul as early as the seventh century BC must only be considered as evidence of trade and not as indicators of social or societal change.

Religion and religious statuary have to be viewed with the same care. Just as a group of people will portray social ideas in architecture and settlement layout, so too will they express religious ideas in sanctuary construction, ideological art, and through ritualistic practice. It is virtually impossible to reconstruct the belief systems of ancient cultures especially when attempting to identify the acculturation of a society which was atectonic and aniconic before contact with the Mediterranean. Even after contacts were established between the Greek colony and the Celtic interior, the art and sanctuary architecture still represent Celtic religious ideas, but use forms which are easier to understand because they are figurative and tangible.

When considering the changing social structures of southern Gallic communities during the seventh to second centuries BC, it becomes clear that, while the manifestation of Gallic culture changed, the underlying structure did not. In short, the southern Gallic Celts do not seem to have absorbed Classical beliefs even after prolonged contact. Instead, new forms, techniques, and methods were used to express their own traditional beliefs and social structure, sometimes leading to the demonstration of a new syncretism – the Gallo-Greeks.

REFERENCES

Abbreviations

CAG 13/2 = F. Gateau and M. Gazenbeek, *Carte archéologique de la Gaule 13/2. Les Alpilles et la Montagnette* (Paris 1999).

EP = D. Ridgeway and F. Ridgeway (eds), *Etruscan Painting. Catalogue Raisonné of Etruscan Wall Painting.* (New York 1986).

FOR = Forma Orbis Romani: Carte archéologique de la Gaule romaine.

MEFRA = Mélanges d'archéologie et d'histoire de l'ecole Française de Rome. Paris.

RIG I = M. Lejeune, *Recuil des Inscriptions Gauloises (R.I.G.) I. Textes gallo-grecs* (Gallia suppl. 45, 1985).

RSL = Revue d'Etudes Ligures.

References

Alexander, J. 1962. "Greeks, Italians, and the Earliest Balkan Iron Age," *Antiquity* 36 (142), pgs. 123-130.

Allen, D.F. 1971. "The Sark hoard." *Archaeologia* 103, pgs. 1-33.

Allen, D.F. 1961. "The Paul (Penzance) hoard of imitation Massilia drachms." *Numismatic Chronicle* 7th *series* (1), pgs. 91-106, pls.XI-XII.

Allen, D.F. 1960. "The origins of coinage in Britain: a reappraisal," in Frere, S.S. (ed) *Problems of the Iron Age in Southern Britain*. London, pgs. 97-308, pls. VII-XVI.

Allen, D.F., and Nash, D. 1980. *The Coins of the Ancient Celts*. Edinburgh.

Amandry, P. 1954. "Autour du cratère grec de Vix," *Revue Archéologique* 43, pgs. 125-140.

Andre, J. 1981. *L'alimentation et la cuisine à Rome*. Les Belles Lettres. Paris.

Andrews, P. 2007. "Springhead: Late Iron Age ceremonial landscape to Roman healing centre?" in R. Haeussler and A.C. King, Continuity and Innovation in Religion in the Roman West, Vol. 1. JRA 67 Rhode Island, pgs. 31-36.

Arcelin, P. 2004. "Les prémices du phénomène urbain à l'âge du Fer en Gaule méridionale. Les agglomérations de la basse vallée du Rhône." *Gallia* 61, pgs. 223-269.

Arcelin, P. 1993a. "Céramique non tournée des ateliers de la région de Marseille," in Py, M. (ed) *Lattara 6: DICOCER. Dictionnaire des céramiques antiques (VIIe s. av. n.è.-VIIe s. de n.è.) en Méditerranée nord-occidentale (Provence, Languedoc, Ampurdan)*, ARALO, Lattes, pgs. 307–310.

Arcelin, P. 1993b. "L'habitat d'Entremont : urbanisme et modes architecturaux," in Coutagne, D. (ed) *Archéologie d'Entremont au Musée Granet*. Aix-en-Provence, pgs. 57-99.

Arcelin, P. 1992a. "Salles hypostyles, portiques et espaces cultuels d'Entremont et de Saint-Blaise (B.-du-Rh.)," *Documents d'Archéologie Méridionale* 15, pgs. 13-27.

Arcelin, P. 1992b. "Société indigène et propositions culturelles massaliotes en basse Provence occidentale," in Bats, et al. (eds) *Marseille grecque et la Gaule (Études Massaliètes 3)*. Lattes, pgs. 305-336.

Arcelin, P. 1990. "Arles," in Arcelin, P. (ed) *Voyage en Massalie. 100 ans d'archéologie en Gaule du Sud*. Marseille, pgs. 194-201.

Arcelin, P. 1987. "Arles Protohistorique," in Sintès, Cl. (dir) *Du nouveau sur l'Arles antique (=Revue d'Arles 1)*, Arles, pgs. 16-27.

Arcelin P., 1971. *La ceramique indigene modelee de Sainte Blaise*. Paris.

Arcelin, P. and Brunaux, J.-L. 2003. *Cultes et sanctuaires en France à l'âge du Fer*. Gallia Supplement 60.

Arcelin, P., and Dedet, B. 1985. "Les encientes protohistoriques du Midi méditerranéen des origines à la fin du Iie s. av. J.-C.," in Dedet, B. and Py, M. (eds) *Les enceintes protohistoriques de Gaule méridionale*. Caveirac, pgs. 11-37.

Arcelin P., Gruat P., et al. 2003. "La France du Sud-Est (Languedoc-Roussillon, Midi-Pyrénées, Provence-Alpes-Côte d'Azur)," in Arcelin, P. and Brunaux, J.-L. *Cultes et sanctuaires en France à l'âge du Fer*. Gallia Supplement 60, pgs. 169-241.

Arcelin, P. and Rouillard, P. 2000. "Premier aperçu sur la composition de la céramique attique d'Arles (B.-du-Rh.) au IVe s. av. J.-C.," in Sabattini, B. (dir) *La céramique attique du IVe siècle en Méditerranée occidentale. Actes du colloque international d'Arles, décembre 1995*. Naples, pgs. 159-165.

Arcelin, P., and Tréziny, H. 1990. "Les habitats indigènes des environs de Marseille grecque," in Arcelin, P. (ed) *Voyage en Massalie : 100 ans d'archéologie en Gaule du Sud*. Marseille, pgs. 26-31.

Arcelin, P., Dedet, B., and Schwaller, M. 1992. "Espaces publics, espaces religieux protohistoriques en Gaule méridionale," in *Espaces et monuments publics protohistoriques de Gaule méridionale*, Documents d'Archéologie Méridionale 15, pgs. 181-242.

Arcelin, P., Pradelle, C., Rigoir, J., and Rigoir, Y. 1983. "Note sur des structures primitives de l'habitat protohistorique de Saint-Blaise (Saint-Mitre-les-Ramparts, B.-du-Rh.)." *Documents d'Archéologie Méridonale* 5, pgs. 138-143.

Arcelin-Pradelle, C. 1984. *La céramique grise monochrome en Provence*. Revue Archéologique de Narbonnaise Supplement 10, Paris.

Arcelin-Pradelle, C., Dedet, B., and Py, M. 1982. "La céramique grise monochrome en Languedoc oriental." *Revue Archéologique de Narbonnaise* 15, pgs. 19–67.

Arnaud, P., and Morena, M. 2004. "À la recherche d'Antipolis grecque: l'apport des opérations récentes," *Collection de l'Ecole française de Rome* 328, pgs. 227-250.

Arnaud-Fassetta, G., and Bourcier, M. 1995. "Mobilité des paysages littoraux et variation du niveau de la mer à Marseille-La Joliette depuis 6000 ans," *Méditerranée* 82 (3,4), pgs. 77-83.

Arnold, B. 1995. "The material culture of social structure: rank and status in early Iron age Europe," in Arnold, B. and Gibson, D.B. (eds) *Celtic chiefdom, Celtic state*. Cambridge, pgs. 43-52.

Arnold, B. and Gibson, D.B. (eds) *Celtic chiefdom, Celtic state*. Cambridge.

Athenaios. *Deipnosophists*. Translation by C.B. Gulick, Loeb Classical Library 1928.

Audouze, F., and Büchsenschütz, O. 1991. *Towns, Villages and Countryside of Celtic Europe*. London.

Agusta-Boularot, S., et al. 2004. "Dix ans de fouilles et recherches à Glanum (Saint-Rémy-de-Provence): 1992-2002." Journal of Roman Archaeology 17, pgs. 26-56.

Avienus, Festus. *Ora Maritima*. Translated by Berthelot, A. Librarie anvienne honoré champion, Paris, 1934.

Barbet, A. 1991. "Roquepertuse et la polychromie en Gaule méridionale à l'époque préromaine." *Documents d'Archéologie Méridionale* 14, pgs. 43-52.

Barruol, G. and Py, M. 1978. "Recherches récentes sur la ville antique d'Espeyran à Saint-Gilles-du-Gard." *Revue Archéologique de Narbonnaise* 11, pgs. 19–100.

Barruol, G., Landes, C., Nickels, A., Py, M., and Roux, J. (eds). 1988. *Lattara I*. Lattes.

Barruol, G. 1969. *Les peuples preromains du sud-est de la Gaule: études de geographie historique*. Paris.

Bats, M. 2006. *Olbia de Provence à l'époque romaine (études Massaliètes 9)*. Aix-en-Provence.

Bats, M. 2004. "Grecs et gallo-grecs, les graffites sur céramique aux sources de l'écriture en Gaule méridionale (IIe-Ier s. av. J. C.)," *Gallia* 61, pgs. 7-20.

Bats, M. 1998. "Marseille archaïque: Étrusques et Phocéens en Méditerranée nord-occidentale," in *Mélanges de l'École Française de Rome, Antiquité* 110, pgs. 609-633.

Bats, M. 1993. "Céramique à pate claire massaliète et de tradition massaliète," in Py, M. (ed) *Lattara 6: Dictionnaire des céramiques antiques (VIIe s. av. n.è.-VIIe s. de n.è.) en Méditerranée nord-occidentale (Provence, Languedoc, Ampurdan)*, ARALO, Lattes, pgs. 206–221.

Bats, M. 1990a. "Colonies et Comptoirs Massaliètes," in Arcelin, P. (ed) *Voyage en Massalie : 100 ans d'archéologie en Gaule du Sud*. Marseille, pgs. 172-175.

Bats, M. 1990b. "Olbia," in Arcelin, P. (ed) *Voyage en Massalie : 100 ans d'archéologie en Gaule du Sud*. Marseille, pgs. 206-213.

Bats, M. (ed) 1990c. *Les amphores de Marseille grecque. Chonologie et diffusion (VIe-Ier s. av. J.-C.) (études Massaliètes 2)*, Lattes.

Bats, M. 1988a. *Vaisselle et alimentation à Olbia de Provence (v. 350-v. 50 av. J.-C.). Modèles culturels et catégories céramiques*. CRNS, Revue Archéologique de Narbonnaise Supplement 18. Paris.

Bats, M. 1988b. "Les inscriptions et graffites sur vases céramiques de Lattara protohistorique (Lattes, Hérault)," in Py, M. (ed) *Lattara 1*, Association pour la Recherche Archéologique en Languedoc Oriental. Lattes, pgs. 147–160.

Bats, M. 1988c. "La logique de l'écriture d'une société à l'autre en Gaule méridionale protohistorique." *Revue Archéologique de Narbonnaise* 21, pgs. 121–148.

Bats, M. 1986. "Le territoire de Marseille grecque: réflexions et problèmes," in Bats, M., and Tréziny, H. (eds) *Le Territoire de Marseille grecque (études Massaliètes 1)*, Aix-en-Provence, pgs. 17–42.

Bats, M. 1979. "Bols hellénistiques à relief trouvés à Olbia en Ligurie (Hyères, Var)." RAN 12, pgs. 161-172.

Bats, M. 1976. "La céramique à vernis noir d'Olbia de Ligurie: vases de l'atelier des petites estampilles." RAN 9, pgs. 63-80.

Bats, M. And Mouchot, D. 1990. "Nice," in Arcelin, P. (ed) *Voyage en Massalie : 100 ans d'archéologie en Gaule du Sud*. Marseille, pgs. 222-225.

Bats, M., and Tréziny, H. (eds). 1986. *Le territoire de Marseille grecque (Actes de la Table-Ronde d'Aix-en-Provence, mars 1985) (études Massaliètes 1)*. Aix-en-Provence.

Batut, M. 1986. *Sorgues, Mourre de Sève, fouille programmée*. Notes d'Information et de Liaison de la Direction des Antiquités de la Région Provence-Alpes-Côte d'Azur 3, pgs. 172–173.

Beazley, J.D. 1956. *Attic black-figure vase-painters*. Oxford.

Benoit, F. 1978. "Cadastrations antiques dans la région d'Agde." *Photo-interprétation*, fasc. 1.

Benoit, F. 1975. "The Celtic oppidum of Entremont, Provence," in Mitford, B. (ed) *Recent archaeological excavations in Europe*. London, pgs. 227-259.

Benoit, F. 1969. *L'art primitif Méditerranéen de la Vallée du Rhône*. Aix-en-Provence.

Benoit, F. 1968. "Résusltats historiques des fouilles d'Entremont (1946-1967)." *Gallia* 26(1), pgs. 1-31.

Benoit, F. 1966. "Topographie antique de Marseille: le théâre et le mur de Crina." *Gallia* 14(1), pgs. 1-20.

Benoit, F. 1965.*Recherches sur l'hellénisation du Midi de la Gaule*. Publications des Annales de la Faculté des Lettres 43, Aix-en-Provence.

Benoit, F. 1957. *Entremont: Capitale Celto-Ligure des Salyens de Provence*. Aix-en-Provence.

Benoit, F. 1945. *L'Art primitif méditerranéen de la Vallée du Rhône-La sculptpure*. Paris.

Bérard, O., Nickels, A., and Schwaller, M. 1990. "Agde," Arcelin, P. (ed) *Voyage en Massalie : 100 ans d'archéologie en Gaule du Sud*. Marseille, pgs. 182-189.

Berthilier-Ajot, N. 1991. "The Vix settlement and the tomb of the princess," in Moscati, et. al (eds) *The Celts*. New York, pgs. 116-117.

Bertucchi, G. 1992. *Les amphores et le vin de Marseille (VIe s. avant J.-C. – IIe s. après J.-C.)*. RAN Supplement XXV. Paris.

Bertucchi, G. 1983. "Amphore et demi-amphore de Marseille au Ier siècle avant J.-C." *Revue Archéologique de Narbonnaise* 16, pgs. 89–102.

Bertucchi, G. 1982. "Fouilles d'urgence et ateliers de potiers sur la butte des Carmes à Marseille: les amphores." *Revue Archéologique de Narbonnaise* 15, pgs. 135–160.

Bertucchi, G., Gantès, L. F., and Tréziny, H. 1995. "Un atelier de coupes ioniennes à Marseille," in Arcelin, P., Bats, M., Garcia, D., Marchand, G., and Schwaller, M. (eds) *Sur les pas des Grecs en Occident (études Massaliètes 4)*, Paris and Lattes, pgs. 367–370.

Bessac, J.-C. 1980. "Le rempart hellénistique de Saint-Blaise (Saint-Mitre-les-Remparts, B.-du-Rh.) : Technique de construction." *Documents d'archéologie méridionale* 3, pgs. 137-157.

Biel, J. 2006. "Eberdingen-Hochdorf, Kr. Ludwigsburg, Baden-Württemberg," *Brathair* 6 (1), pgs. 3-9.

Biel, J. 1991. "The Celtic princes of Höhenasperg (Baden-Württemberg)," in Moscati, et. al (eds) *The Celts*. New York, pgs. 108-113.

Biel, J. 1987. "A Celtic grave in Hochdorf, Germany," *Archaeology* 40 (6), pgs. 22-29.

Biel, J. 1985. *Der Keltenfurst von Hochdorf*. Stuttgart.

Biel, J. 1981. "The late Hallstatt chieftain's grave at Hochdorf," *Antiquity* 55 (213), pgs. 16-18.

Blanchet, A. 1905. *Traité des monnaies Gauloise*. Paris.

Boardman, J. 1964. *The Greeks overseas*. Harmondsworth.

Bober, P. 1948. "Review: Fouilles de Glanum (Saint-Remy-de-Provence). *American Journal of Archaeology* 52(3), pgs. 410-411.

Boissinot, P. 2001. "Archéologie des vignobles antiques du sud de la Gaule." *Gallia* 58, pgs. 45-68.

Boissinot, P. 1995. "L'empreinte des paysages helléniques dans les formations holocènes de Saint-Jean du Désert (Marseille)." *Méditerranée* 82(3.4), pgs. 33–40.

Bonifay, M., and Tréziny, H. 1995. "Marseille: Jardin des Vestiges de la Bourse," *Bilan Scientifique, Direction Régionale des Affaires Culturelles, Service Régionale de l'Archéologie, Provence-Alpes-Côte d'Azur* 1994, pgs. 137-138.

Bouby, L., and Marnival, P. 2001. "La vigne et les débuts de la viticulture en France: appports de l'archéobotanique." *Gallia* 58, pgs. 13-28.

Bouloumié, B. 1990. "L'épave étrusque d'Antibes," Arcelin, P. (ed) *Voyage en Massalie : 100 ans d'archéologie en Gaule du Sud*. Marseille, pgs. 42-45.

Bouloumié, B. 1984. "Un oppidum gaulois à Saint-Blaise en Provence," *Les Dossiers: histoire et archéologie* 84, pgs. 6-96.

Bouloumié, B. 1979. "Saint-Blaise. Note sommaire sur cinq années de fouilles et de recherches," *Gallia* 37, pgs. 229-236.

Bouloumié, B. 1978. "Les tumulus de Pertuis (Vaucluse) et les oenochoés rhodiennes hors d'Etrurie." *Gallia* 36, pgs. 219-240.

Bouloumie B. 1976. "Les amphores etrusques de Saint Blaise." *Revue Archéologique de Narbonnaise* 9, pgs 23-43.

Bouloumié, B., and Borély, B. 1992. *Saint-Blaise (Fouilles H. Rolland): L'habitat protohistorique les céramiques grecques*. Provence.

Bouiron, M. 1995. "Le fond du Vieux-Port à Marseille, des marécages à la place Général-de-Gaulle," *Méditerranée* 82(3.4): 63–69.

Bouscaras, A. 1954. "Recherche sous-marine au large d'Agde (1951-53)." *RSL* XX 1, pgs. 47-54.

Brien-Poitevin, F. 1990. "Tauroeis," Arcelin, P. (ed) *Voyage en Massalie : 100 ans d'archéologie en Gaule du Sud*. Marseille, pgs. 202-205.

Brenot, C. 1990. "Le monnayage de Marseille de la fin du IIIe siècle à 49 avant J.-C.," in Duval, A., Morel, J. P., and Roman, Y. (eds) *Gaule interne et Gaule méditerranéenne aux IIe et Ier siècles avant J.-C.: confrontations chronologiques*. CRNS, Revue Archéologique de Narbonnaise Supplement 21. Paris, pgs. 27–35.

Brenot, C. 1989. "Un trésor de monnaies de Marseille decouvert sur le site de La Courtine d'Ollioules." *Bulletin de la Société Nationale des Antiquaries de France*.

Brogan, O. 1958. "Review: Fouilles de Saint-Blaise," *American Journal of Archaeology* 62 (3), pgs. 348-349.

Brun, J.-P. 2004. *Archéologie du vin et de l'huile dans l'Empire Romain*. Paris.

Brun, J.-P. 1993. "L'oléiculture et la viticulture antique en Gaule: instruments et installations de production," in Amouretti, M. C., and Brun, J. P. (eds) *La production du vin et de l'huile en Méditerranée*. Correspondence Hellénique Supplement 26, Paris, pgs. 307–341.

Brun, J.-P. 1992. "Le village massaliote de la Galère à Porquerolles (Var) et la géographie des *stoechades* au 1er s. av. J.-C.," in Bats, M., Bertucchi, G., Congès, G., and Tréziny, H. (eds.),Marseille grecque et la Gaule (études Massaliètes 3), ADAM Editions, Lattes, pp. 279-288.

Brun, J.-P., Charrière, J.-L., Congès, G. 1998. "L'huilerie de l'îlot III et les pressoirs d'Entremont." *Documents d'Archéologie méridionale,* 21, pgs. 44-57.

Büchsenschütz, O. 1995. "The significance of major settlements in European Iron Age society," in Arnold, B. and Gibson, D.B. (eds) *Celtic chiefdom, Celtic state*. Cambridge, pgs. 53-63.

Büchsenschütz, O. 1984. *Structures d'habitats et fortifications de l'Age du Fer en France Septentrionale*. Paris.

Burgess, J.S. 2004. *The tradition of the Trojan War in Homer and the Epic Cycle*. Baltimore.

Buxó i Capdevila, R. 1996. "Evidence for vines and ancient cultivation from an urban area, Lattes (Hérault), southern France." *Antiquity* 70, pgs. 393-407.

Buxó i Capdevila, R. 1993. *Des semences et des fruits: cueillette et agriculture en France et en Espagne méditerranéennes du Néolithique à l'Age du Fer.* Unpublished PhD Thesis, Université de Montpellier II.

Caesar, Julius. *The Civil War*. Penguin Classics, 2004.

Carcopino, J. 1957. *Promenades historiques aux pays de*

la Dame de Vix. Paris.

Castabyer, P., Sanmarti, E., Tremoleda, J. 1993. "Atelier des petites estampilles," in Py, M. (ed) *Lattara 6: Dictionnaire des céramiques antiques (VIIe s. av. n.è.-VIIe s. de n.è.) en Méditerranée nord-occidentale (Provence, Languedoc, Ampurdan)*. Association pour la Recherche Archéologique en Languedoc Oriental, Lattes, pgs. 525–526.

Chabal, L. 1991. *L'homme et l'évolution de la végétation méditerranéenne, des ages des métaux à la période romaine: recherches anthracologiques théoriques appliqués principalement à des sites du Bas-Languedoc.* Monograph?, Université de Montpellier II.

Chabal, L. 1982. *Méthodes de prélèvement des bois carbonisés protohistoriques pour l'étude des relations homme-végétation (exemple d'un habitat de l'Age du Fer : Le Marduel).* D.E.A., U.S.T.L.-Montpellier II.

Charles-Picard, G. 1963. "Glanum et les origines de l'art romano-provençal: première partie, architecture," *Gallia* 21, pgs. 111-124.

Charmasson, J. 1967. "La Pénétration de l'hellénisme par les vallées de la Tave et de la Cèze, Gard aux VIème-Vème s. avant J. C. : les sites hellénisés de Gaujac Montfaucon et Saint-Laurent de Carnols." *Ogam* 19, pgs.145-168.

Chausserie-Laprée, J. and Nin, N. 1990. "Le village protohistorique du quartier de l'Ile à Martigues (B.-du-Rh.). Les espaces domestiques de la phase primitive (début Vème-début Iième s. av. J.-C.). I. Les aménagements domestiques," *Documents d'Archéologie Méridionale* 13, pgs. 35-136.

Chausserie-Laprée, J. and Nin, N. 1987. "Le village protohistorique du quartier de l'Ile à Martigues (B.-du-Rh.). Urbanisme et architecture de la phase primitive (début Vème-début Iième s. av. J.-C.). II. Données nouvelles sur l'urbanisme et architecture domestique," *Documents d'Archéologie Méridionale* 10, pgs. 31-89.

Chausserie-Laprée, J., Nin, N., and Comallain, L. 1984. "Le village protohistorique du quartier de l'Ile à Martigues (B.-du-Rh.). Urbanisme et architecture de la phase primitive (Vème-IIIème s. av. J.-C.). I. Urbanisme et fortifications," *Documents d'Archéologie Méridionale* 7, pgs. 27-52.

Chazelles, C. and Roux, J.-C. 1988. "L'emploi des adobes dans l'aménagement de l'habitat à Lattes, au IIIe s. av. n. è. : les sols et les banquettes." In Py. M. (ed) *Lattara 1.* Lattes, pgs. 161-174.

Clavel-Lévêque, M. 1982. "Un cadastre grec en Gaule: la chora d'Agde (Hérault)." *Klio* 64, pgs. 21–28.

Clavel-Lévêque, M. 1977. *Marseille grecque: la dynamique d'un impérialisme marchand.* Marseille.

Clavel-Lévêque, M., and Mallart, R. P. 1995. *Cité et territoire. Colloque Européen, Béziers, 14-16 octobre, 1994.* Paris.

Clavel-Lévêque, M., and Vignot, A. 1998. *Cité et territoire. Colloque Européen, Béziers, 24-26 octobre, 1997.* Paris.

Clerc, M. 1930. *Massalia. Histoire de Marseille dans l'Antiquite, des origines a la fin de l'Empire romain d'Occident 2 vols. (Marseille 1927-1929).* Marseille.

Clergues, J.H. 1969. *Antibes: la ville grecque du VIe siècle avant Jésus-Christ et l'habitat protohistorique.* Antibes.

Colbert de Beaulieu, J.B. and Richard, J.-C.M. 1970. "La numismatique de la Gaule et la numismatique de la Narbonnaise," in *Hommage à F. Benoît* III, RSL, pgs. 90-100.

Collis, J. 1984. *Oppida: Earliest Towns North of the Alps.* Sheffield.

Conche, F. 1996. "Marseille: Rue Jean-François Leca, 9." *Bilan Scientifique 1995, Direction Régionale des Affaires Culturelles, Service Régional de l'Archéologie, Provence-Alpes-Côte d'Azur,* pgs. 159–161.

Congès, G. 1990. "Entremont," Arcelin, P. (ed) *Voyage en Massalie : 100 ans d'archéologie en Gaule du Sud.* Marseille, pgs. 154-155.

Cook, R.M. 1997. *Greek painted pottery.* London.

Creed, G. 2006. *Seductions of community: emancipations, oppressions, quandaries.* Santa Fe.

Cunliffe, B. 2001. *Facing the ocean: the Atlantic and its peoples.* Oxford.

Cunliffe, B. 1988. *Greeks, Romans and Barbarians: spheres of interaction.* London.

Déchelette, J. 1914. Manuel d'archéologie préhistorique, celtique et gallo-romaine, II, 3, second Age du Fer ou époque de La Tène. Paris.

Dedet, B. 1999. "La Maison de l'oppidum languedocien durant la Protohistoire : forme et utilisation de l'espace." *Gallia* 56, pgs. 313-355.

Dedet, B. 1990. "Une maison à absides sur l'oppidum de Gailhan (Gard) au milieu du Ve s. avant J.-C. : la question du plan absidial en Gaule du Sud." *Gallia* 47, pgs. 29-55.

Dedet, B. 1987. *Habitat et vie quotidienne en Languedoc au milieu de L'Age du Fer: l'unité domestique no. 1 de Gailhan, Gard.* CRNS, Revue Archéologique de Narbonnaise Supplement 17. Paris.

Dedet, B. 1980. *Premières recherches sur l'oppidum du Plan de la Tour à Gailhan, Gard, Sondages 1975-1977.* Association pour la Recherche Archéologique en Languedoc Oriental, Caveirac.

Dedet, B., Py, M., and Savay-Guerraz, H. (eds). 1985. *L'occupation des rivages de l'Etang de Mauguio (Hérault) au Bronze final et au Premier Age du Fer, Vols. 2 and 3.* Association pour la Recherche Archéologique en Languedoc Oriental, Cahier 12. Caveirac.

Dehn, W. 1958. "Die Befestigung der Heuneberg (Per. IV) und die griechische Mittelmeerwelt," in Martin, R. *Actes du Colloque sur les influences helléniques en Gaule.* Dijon, pgs. 55-62.

Dehn, W., and Frey, O.H. 1962. "Die absolute chronologie der Hallstatt- und Frühlatènezeit Mitteleuropas grund deas Südimports," *Atti del VI congresso internazionale delle scienze preistoriche e protostoriche.* Florence, pgs. 197-208.

Derks, T. 1998. *Gods, temples, and ritual practices: the transformation of religious ideas and values in Roman Gaul.* Amsterdam.

Dietler, M. 1997. "The Iron Age in Mediterranean France: Colonial encounters, entanglements, and transformations," *Journal of World Prehistory* 11 (3), pgs. 269-358.

Dietler, M. 1990. *Exchange, Consumption, and Colonial Interaction in the Rhône Basin of France: A Study of Early Iron Age Political Economy, (2 Vols.).* Ph.D. dissertation, University of California, Berkeley.

Dietler, M. 1995. "Early 'Celtic' socio-political relations: ideological representation and social competition in dynamic comparative perspective," in Arnold, B. and Gibson, D.B. (eds) *Celtic chiefdom, Celtic state.* Cambridge, pgs. 64-71.

Dietler, M., and Herbich, I. (1998). "Habitus, techniques, style: An integrated approach to the social understanding of material culture and boundaries," In Stark, M. (ed), *The Archaeology of Social Boundaries.* Washington, DC, pgs. 232-263.

Dietler, M., and Herbich, I. (1993). "Living on Luo time: Reckoning sequence, duration, history, and biography in a rural African society," *World Archaeology* (25), pgs. 248-260.

Diodorus. *Library of History.* Translation by C.H. Oldfather, Harvard Loeb 1989.

Dominguez, A. 2004. "Spain and France (including Corsica)," in Hansen, M.H., and Nielsen, T.H. (eds) *An inventory of the archaic and classical poleis.* Oxford, pgs. 157-171.

Driehaus, J. 1966. "Zur Verbreitung der eisenzeitlichen Situlen im mittelrheinischen Gebirgsland," *Bonner Jahrb.* 166, pgs. 26-47.

Drinkwater, J.F. *Roman Gaul: the three provinces 58 BC - AD 260.* London.

Ducat, J. and Farnoux, B.C. 1976. "Origines grecques et romaines," in Bordes, M. (ed) *Histoire de Nice et du pays niçois,* Toulouse, pgs. 9-54.

Duprat, E.H. 1936. "Tauroentum, Six Fours, Var," *Institut historique de Provence,* Marseille.

Ebel, C. 1976. *Transalpine Gaul: the emergence of a Roman province.* Leiden.

Eluère, C. 1991. "The Celts and their gold," in Moscati, et. al (eds) *The Celts.* New York, pgs. 349-355.

Eluère, C. 1990. *Les secrets de l'or antique.* Paris.

Eluère, C. 1987a. *L'or des Celtes.* Paris.

Eluère, C. 1987b. "Celtic gold torcs." *Gold Bulletin* 20 (1/2), pgs. 22-37.

Eluère, C., et al. 1989. Bulletin de la Société Préhistorique Francaise 86, pgs. 107-121.

Erroux, J. 1987. "Étude des vestiges paléobotaniques (plantes cultivées et pépins de raisin)," in Dedet, B. *Habitat et vie quotidienne en Languedoc au milieu de l'Age du Fer: l'unité domestiqque n°1 de Gailhan, Gard.* Revue Archéologique Narbonnaise Supplement 17, pgs. 225-228.

Erroux, J. 1980a. "Étude des vestiges paléo-botaniques (plantes cultivées et pépins de raisin)," in Dedet, B. *Premières recherches sur l'oppidum du Plan de la Tour à Gailhan, Gard, sondages 1975-1977.* Association pur la Recherche de l'Archéologie Orientale 5, pgs. 117-122.

Erroux, J. 1980b. "Étude d'un échantillon de graines carbonisées provenant du site de La Lagaste à Rouffiac-d'Aude," in Rancoule, G. *La Lagaste, agglomeration gauloise du basin de l'Aude.* Atacina 10, pgs. 138-139.

Eschallier, J.C. 1991. "Common and Pseudo-Ionian ware from le Pegue (Drôme, France): An analytical and archaeological problem," in Middleton, A. and Freestone, I (eds) *Recent developments in ceramic petrology. British Museum occasional paper no. 81.* London.

Euzennat, M. 1980. "Ancient Marseilles in the light of recent excavations." *American Journal of Archaeology* 84, pgs. 133–140.

Fabre, G. 1934. "Une maison a peristyle a Glanum," REA 36, pgs. 366-379.

Fernandez, J.W. 1977. *Fang Architectonics.* Philadelphia.

Feugère, M., and Guillot, A. 1986. "Fouilles de Bragny, 1: les petits objets dans leur contexte du Hallstatt final." *Revue Archéoloqique de l'Est et du Centre-Est* 37, pgs. 159–221.

Février, P. 1973. "The origin and growth of the cities of Southern Gaul to the third century A.D.: an assessment of the most recent archaeological discoveries," *Journal of Roman Studies* 63, pgs. 1-28.

Fillières, D. 1978. *Contribution à l'étude de la production et de l'exportation des amphores dites marseillaises et des céramiques grecques d'Occident du Midi de la France au moyen d'analyses par activation neutronique avec traitement taxinomique des résultats.* Unpublished doctoral dissertation, Université de Paris I, Paris.

Fischer, F. 1995. "The early Celts of west central Europe: the semantics of social structure," in Arnold, B. and Gibson, D.B. (eds) *Celtic chiefdon, Celtic state.* Cambridge, pgs. 34-40.

Fischer, F. 1991. "Kleinaspergle near Asperg," in Moscati, et. al (eds) *The Celts.* New York, pgs. 178-179.

Frankenstein, S., and Rowlands, M.J. 1978. "The internal structure and regional context of Early Iron Age society in South-western Germany," *Bull. Inst. Archaeol. Univ. London* 15, pgs. 73-112.

Frey, O.H. 1991a. "Celtic Princes," in Moscati, et. al (eds) *The Celts.* New York, pgs. 75-92.

Frey, O.H. 1991b. "The formation of the La Téne culture in the fifth century B.C." in Moscati, et al. (eds) *The Celts.* New York, pgs. 127-146.

Furtwängler, A. E. 1978.*Monnaies grecques en Gaule. Le trésor d'Auriol et le monnayage de Massalia 525/520-460 av. J.-C.,* Office du Livre, Fribourg.

Gagnière, S., and Granier, J. 1962. "Les niveaux historiques de la grotte du Lierre à Saint-Genies-de-Comolas (Gard)." *Provence historique* 12, pgs. 173-188.

Gaiffe, O. 1985. "La céramique grise à décor ondé dans le Centre-Est de la France: l'apport du Camp de Chassey." *Revue Archéologique de l'Est et du Centre-Est* 36, pgs. 221–224.

Gailledrat, E. 1993a. "Céramique peinte ibéro-languedocienne," in Py, M. (ed) *Lattara 6: Dictionnaire des céramiques antiques (VIIe s. av. n.è.-VIIe s. de n.è.) en Méditerranée nord-occidentale (Provence, Languedoc, Ampurdan).* Association pour la Recherche Archéologique en Languedoc Oriental, Lattes, pgs. 461–469.

Gailledrat, E. 1993b. "Les céramiques peintes ibériques au Ve siècle avant J.-C. en Languedoc occidental et en Roussillon." *Documents d'Archéologie Méridionale* 16, pgs. 64–79.

Gailledrat, É., and Marchand, G. 2003. "Sigean (Aude). Pech Maho. Un ensemble à caractère public et cultuel dans l'habitat," in Arcelin, P., and Brunaux, J.-L., (eds), *Cultes et sanctuaires en France à l'âge du Fer. Gallia*

60 Dossier, pgs. 234-238.

Gallet de Santerre, H. 1980. *Ensérune, les silos de la terrasse est.* Paris.

Gallet de Santerre, H. 1977. "La diffusion de la céramique attique aux Ve et IVe siècles av. J.-C. sur les rivages français de la Méditerranée." Revue Archéologique de Narbonnaise 10, pgs. 33-57.

Gallet de Santerre, H. 1964. "Informations archéologiques du Languedoc." *Gallia* 22, pgs. 502-504.

Gantès, L.-F. 1992a. La topographie de Marseille grecque. Bilan des recherches (1829–1991). In Bats, M., Bertucchi, G., Congès, G., and Tréziny, H. (eds.),Marseille grecque et la Gaule (études Massaliètes 3), ADAM Editions, Lattes, pp. 71–88.

Gantès, L. -F. 1992b. "L'apport des fouilles récentes à l'étude quantitative de l'économie massaliète," in Bats, M., Bertucchi, G., Congès, G., and Tréziny, H. (eds.),Marseille grecque et la Gaule (études Massaliètes 3), ADAM Editions, Lattes, pp. 171–178.

Gantès, L.-F. 1990. *Massalia retrouvée.* Les Dossiers d'Archéologie 154: 14–21

Gantès, L.-F., and Moliner, M. 1990.*Marseille, itinéraire d'une mémoire. Cinq années d'archéologie municipale.* Musée d'histoire de Marseille, Marseille.

Garcia, D. 2004. *La celtique méditerranéene. Habitats et sociétés en Languedoc et en Provence, VIIIe-Iie siècles av. J.-C.* Paris.

Garcia, D. 2002. "Épave de Rochelongue (Cap d'Agde)," in Long, L., Pomey, P. and Sourisseau, J.-C. (eds) *Les Etrusques en Mer. Épaves d'Antibes à Marseille*, Aix-en-Provence, pgs. 38–41.

Garcia, D. 1995. "Le territoire d'Agde grecque et l'occupation du sol en Languedoc central durant l'Age du Fer," In Arcelin, P., Bats, M., Garcia, D., Marchand, G., and Schwaller, M. (eds) *Sur les pas des Grecs en Occident (Études Massaliètes 4).* Paris, pgs. 137-167.

Garcia, D. (ed). 1994. *Lattara 7: Exploration de la ville portuaire de Lattes. Les îlots 2, 4-sud, 5, 7-est, 7-ouest, 8, 9 et 16 du quartier Saint-Sauveur.* Lattes.

Garcia, D. 1993. *Entre Ibères et Ligures. Lodévois et moyenne vallée de l'Hérault protohistoriques.* CNRS, Revue Archéologique de Narbonnaise. Paris.

Garcia, D. 1992a. "Du grain et du vin, à propos des structures de stockage de l'agglomération portuaire de Lattes," in Py, M. (ed) *Lattara 5.* Lattes, pgs. 165-182.

Garcia, D. 1992b. "Les elements de pressoirs de Lattes et l'oléculture antique en Languedoc méditerranéen." in Py, M. (ed) *Lattara 5.* Lattes, pgs. 237-258.

Garcia, D. 1990. "Urbanisme et architecturede la ville de Lattara aux Iie-Ier s. av. n. è. Premiers observations." *Lattara* 3, pgs. 303-316.

Garcia, D., and Marchand, G. 1995. "A propos du faciès céramique d'Agde (Hérault)," Arcelin, P., Bats, M., Garcia, D., Marchand, G., and Schwaller, M. (eds) *Sur les pas des Grecs en Occident (Études Massaliètes 4).* Paris, pgs 99-103.

Garcia, D., and Orliac, C. 1993. "La vallée de l'Hérault durant la protohistoire," *Bulletin du Groupe de Recherches et d'Études du Clemontais* 67-69, pgs. 23-32.

Gascou, J. 1994. "Caunes-Minervois, l'enciente du Cros," *Bilan Scientifique 1993, direction régionale des affaires culturelles, Service régional de l'archéologie, Provence-Alpes-Côte d'Azur Laguedoc-Roussillon*, pgs. 41-42.

Gateau, F., and Provost, M. 1996. *Carte archéologique de la Gaule: L'Etang de Berre 13/1.* L'Académie des Inscriptions et Belles-Lettres. Paris.

Gellius, Aulus. *Noctes Atticae. Tomus I, Libri 1-10.* Clarendon Press 1990.

Gentric, G. 1981.*Circulation monétaire dans la basse vallée du Rhône (IIe-Ier s. av. J.-C.) d'après les monnaies de Bollène (Vaucluse).* Association pour la Recherche Archéologique en Languedoc Oriental, Caveirac.

Gérin-Ricard, H. 1927. *Le sanctuarie préromain de Roquepertuse à Velaux (Bouches-du-Rhône).* Marseille.

Giry, A. 1974. *L'oppidum d'Ensérune.* Salles-d'Aude.

Giry, J. 1961. *Les fouilles de Montlaurès.* Bulletin de la Commission Archéologique de Narbonne 25. Narbonne.

Goodman, P. 2007. *The Roman city and its periphery: from Rome to Gaul.* London.

Goudineau, C. 1991. "Les sanctuaires gaulois : relecture d'inscriptions et de textes," in Brunaux, J.-L. (ed) *Les sanctuaires celtiques et leurs rapports avec le monde méditerranéen, Actes du colloque de Saint-Riquier, 8-11 nov. 1990.* Paris, pgs. 250-256.

Goudineau, C. 1984. "Un contrepoids de pressoir à huile d'Entremont (Bouches-du-Rhône)." *Gallia* 42, pgs. 219-221.

Goudineau, C. 1983. "Marseilles, Rome and Gaul from the third to the first century BC," in Garnsey, P., Hopkins, K., Whittaker, C.R. (eds) *Trade in the Ancient Economy.* London, pgs. 76-86.

Goury, D. 1995. "Les vases pseudo-ioniens des vallées de la Cèze et de la Tave (Gard)," in Arcelin, P., Bats, M., Garcia, D., Marchand, G., and Schwaller, M. (ed) *Sur les pas des Grecs en Occident (études Massaliètes 4).* Paris and Lattes, pgs. 309–324.

Graham, A.J. 2001. "Pre-colonial Contacts: Questions and Problems," in Graham, A.J. *Collected Papers on Greek Colonization*, pgs. 25-44.

Gran-Aymerich, J. 1997. "Les premières importations méditerannéennes de Bourges," in Brun, P. and Chaume, B. (eds) *Vix et les éphémères principautés celtiques. Les Vie-Ve siècle savant J.-C. en Europe centre-occidentale.* Actes du colloque de Châtillon-sur-Seine (27-29 Octobre 1993). Paris, pgs. 201-212.

Green, M. (ed). 1995. *The Celtic world.* London.

Green, M. 1989. *Symbol and Image in Celtic Religious Art.* London.

Grierson, P. 1978. The origins of money. *Research in Economic Anthropology* 1, pgs. 1–35.

Gros, P. and Varène, P. 1984. "La forum et la basilique de Glanum : problèmes de chronologie et de restitution." *Gallia*, pgs. 21-52.

Guerra, M.F., and Calligaro, T. 2003. "Gold cultural heritage objects: a review of studies of provenance and manufacturing technologies. *Measurement Science and Technology* 14, pgs. 1527-1537.

Guery, R. 1992. "Le port antique de Marseille," in Bats, M., Bertucchi, G., Congès, G., and Tréziny, H. (eds*), Marseille grecque et la Gaule (études Massaliètes 3)*, Lattes, pgs. 109–121.

Guilaine, J. And Ayme, R. 1960. "Sondage à la grotte des

Chambres d'Alaric (Moux, Aude)." *Cahiers ligures de prèhistoire et d'archéologie*, pgs. 139-146.

Guy, M. 1995. "Cadastres en bandes de Métaponte à Agde. Questions et methods," in Arcelin, P., Bats, M., Garcia, D., Marchand, G., and Schwaller, M. (eds), *Sur les pas des Grecs en Occident (études Massaliètes 4)*, Paris and Lattes, pgs. 427–444.

Haeussler, R. 2007. "The dynamics and contradictions of religious change in Gallia Narbonensis," in Haeussler, R. and King, A.C. (eds) *Continuity and innovation in religion in the Roman West, Volume 1*. JRS 67, pgs. 81-102.

Hansen, M.H., and Nielsen, T.H. 2004. *An inventory of the archaic and classical poleis*. Oxford.

Harding, D.W. 2007. *The archaeology of Celtic art*. New York.

Haselgrove, C. 1978. *Supplementary gazetteer of find-spots of Celtic coins in Britain, 1977*. Institute of Archaeology occasional paper no. 11a. London.

Hawkes, C.F.C. 1963. "The Celts: report on the study of their culture and their Mediterranean relations, 1942-1962," in Demargne (ed) *VIIIe Congrès Int. D'Archéologie classique: rapports et communications*. Paris, pgs. 3-23.

Haywood, J. 2001. *Historical atlas of the Celtic World*. London.

Herbich, I., and Dietler, M. 1993. "Space, time, and symbolic structure in the Luo homestead: an ethnoarchaeological study of "settlement biography" in Africa," in Pavúk, J (ed) *Actes du XIIe Congrès International des Sciences Préhistoriques et Protohistoriques, Bratislava, Czechoslovakia, September 1-7, 1991, vol. 1*. Nitra, pgs. 26-32.

Herodotus. The Histories. Translation by A. De Sélincourt, Penguin Books 1996.

Hermary, A., Hesnard, A., and Tréziny, H. 1999. *Marseille Grecque. La cité phocéenne (600-49 av. J.-C.)*. Errance.

Hesnard, A. 1995. "Les ports antiques de Marseille, Place Jules-Verne." *Journal of Roman Archaeology* 8, pgs. 65–77.

Hesnard, A. 1994. "Une nouvelle fouille du port de Marseille, place Jules-Verne." *Comptes rendus de l'Academie des Inscriptions et Belles-Lettres* Janvier–Mars, pgs. 195–217.

Hesnard, A. 1993. Place Jules-Verne, in *Le temps des découvertes. Marseille de Protis à la reine Jeanne*. Musées de Marseille, Marseille, pgs. 55–59.

Hodson, F.R. and Rowlett, R.M. 1973. "From 600 B.C. to the Roman conquest," in Piggott, S., Daniel, G. and McBurney, C. (eds) *France before the Romans*. London, pgs. 157-191.

Houlès, N. and Janin, Th. 1992. "Une tombe du premier Age du Fer au lieu-dit Saint-Antoine à Castelnau-de-Guers, Hérault." RAN 25, pgs. 433-441.

Jacobsthal, P. 1944. *Early Celtic Art*. Oxford.

Jannoray, J. *Ensérune. Contribution a l'étude des civilisations préromaines de la Gaule méridionale*. Paris.

De Jersey, P. 1999. "Exotic Celtic coinage in Britain." *Journal of Archaeology* 18 (2), pgs. 189-216.

Joffroy, R. 1960. *L'Oppidum de Vix et la civilisation hallstattienne finale dans l'Est de la France*. Paris.

Joffroy, R. 1958. *Les Séputures à char du premier âge du fer en France*. Paris.

Joffroy, R. 1954. *Le tresor de Vix (Côte d'Or)*. Paris.

Jones, H.S. 1894. "The Chest of Kypselos." *Journal of Hellenic Studies* 14, pgs. 30-80.

Jope, M. 1995. "The Social Implications of Celtic Art: 600BC to AD 600," in Miranda Green (ed), *The Celtic World*. London, 376-410.

Jully, J. J. 1983. *Céramiques grecques ou de type grec et autres céramiques en Languedoc méditerranéen, Roussillon et Catalogne VIIe-IVe s. avant notre ère, et leur contexte socio-culturel*. ii/1. Paris.

Jully, J.-J. 1980. *Les importations de céramique attique (Vie-Ive s.) en Languedoc méditerranéen, Roussillon et Catalogne*. Paris.

Jully, J. J., and Nordström, S. 1972. "Une forme de céramique ibéro-languedocienne: la jarre bitronconique." *Archivo de Prehistoria Levantina* 13, pgs. 93–101.

Kearns, E. 1989. *The heroes of Attica*. London.

Kellner, H.-J. 2000. "Coinage," in Kruta, V., et al. (eds) *The Celts*. New York, pgs. 475-484.

Kimmig, W. 1991. "The Heuneberg hillfort and the Proto-Celtic princely tombs of Upper Rhineland," in Moscati, et. al (eds) *The Celts*. New York, pgs. 114-115.

Kimmig, W. 1988. *Das Kleinaspergle. Studien zu einem Fürstengrabhügel der frühen Latènezeit bei Stuttgart*. Stuttgart.

Kimmig, W. 1975. "Early Celts on the upper Danube: the excavations at the Heuneberg," in Mitford, B. (ed) *Recent archaeological excavations in Europe*. London, pgs. 32-64.

Kimmig, W. 1968. *Die Heuneburg an der oberen Donau*. Stuttgart.

Kimmig, W. 1958. "Kulturbeziehungen zwischen der Nordwestalpinen Hallstattkultur und der Mediteranean Welt," in Martin, R. *Actes du Collogque sur les influences helléniques en Gaule*. Dijon, pgs. 75-87.

Kimmig, W., and Gersbach, R. 1971. "Die Grabungen auf der Heuneberg 1966-1969," *Germania* 49, pgs. 21-91.

King, A. 1990. *Roman Gaul and Germany*. London.

Lagrand, C. 1987. "Le Premier Age du Fer dans le Sud-Est de la France," *Hallstatt-Studien (Tübinger Kolloquium zur westeuropäischen Hallstatt-Zeit 1980)*, VCH Acta Himaopra Weinheim, pgs. 44-88.

Lagrand, C. 1986. "Les habitats de Tamaris, l'Arquet et Saint-Pierre à Martigues," in Bats, M., and Tréziny, H. (eds) *Le territoire de Marseille grecque. (Études Massaliètes 1)*, Aix-en-Provence, pgs. 127-135.

Lagrand, C. 1981. "Le territoire de Martigues au Bronze final et à l'Age du Fer," *Quatrième centenaire de l'union des trous quartiers de Martigues*. Marseille, pgs, 39-54.

Lagrand, C. 1979. "Un nouvel habitat de la période de colonisation grecque : Saint-Pierre-lès-Martigues (Bouches-du-Rhône) (Vième s. av. J.-C.-Ier s. ap. J.-C.)," *Documents d'Archéologie Méridonale* 2, pgs. 81-106.

Lagrand, C. 1968. *Recherches sur le Bronze final en Provence méridionale*. Thèse d'Université, Aix-en-Provence.

Lagrand, C. 1959. "Un habitat côtier de l'Age du Fer à L'Arquet, à La Couronne (Bouches-du-Rhône)," *Gallia* 17, pgs. 179-201.

Lagrand, C., and Thalmann, J.-P. 1973. *Les habitats protohistoriques du Pègue (Drôme), le sondage no. 8 (1957–1971)*. Centre de Documentation de la Préhistoire Alpine, Cahier 2, Grenoble.

Lambert, P.-Y. 1992. "Diffusion de l'écriture gallo-grecque en milieu indigène," in Bats, M., Bertucchi, G., Congès, G., and Tréziny, H. (eds.) *Marseille grecque et la Gaule (études Massaliètes 3)*, ADAM Editions, Lattes, pp. 289–294.

Landes, C., Cayzac, N., Laissac, V., and Millet, F. 2003. *Les Etrusques en France*. Lattes.

Latour, J. 1985. "L'oppidum du Baou-des-Noirs à Vence (A.-M.)," *Documents d'Archéologie Méridonale* 8, pgs. 9-24.

Layat, J. 1959. "Tauroentum était au Brusc," *Bulletin de l'Académie du Var*.

Layet, J. 1949a. *La Courtine d'Ollioules, capitale agricole de la future région toulonnaise entre le VIIè et la fin de IIè siècle avant notre ère*. Toulon.

Layet, J. 1949b. *Le sanctuaire celto-ligure, l'huilerie et le nouveau quartier de maisons de l'oppidum de la Courtine, campagne de fouilles 1947-1948*. Toulon.

Lejeune, M. 1985. *Textes gallo-grecs (Recueil des Inscriptions Gauloises, Vol. 1)*. CNRS Editions, Paris.

Lejeune, M. 1983. "Rencontre de l'alphabet grec avec les langues barbares au cours du Ier millénaire avant J.-C," in *Modes de contacts et processus de transformation dans les sociétés anciennes*. école Française de Rome, Rome, pgs. 731–753.

Leroy, M. et al. 2000. "La sidérurgie dans l'Est de la Gaul," *Gallia* 57, pgs. 11-21.

Lescure, B. 1991. "The hillfort and sanctuary at Roquepertuse," in Moscati, et al. (ed) *The Celts*. New York, pgs. 362-363.

Leveau, P., Heinz, C., Laval, H., Marinval, P., Medus, J. 1991. "Les origines de l'oléculture en Gaule du sud, Données historiques, archéologiques et botaniques." *Revue de Archéometrie* 15, pgs. 83-94.

Livy. *The Rise of Rome : books one – five*. Translation by T.J. Luce, Oxford University Press 1998.

Lomas, K. 2006. "Beyond Magna Graecia : Greeks and Non-Greeks in France, Spain and Italy," in Kinzl, K.H. (ed) *A companion to the classical Greek world*. Oxford, pgs. 174-196.

Long, L. 2002. "Epave de La Love (Cap d'Antibes)," in Long, L., Pomey, P. et Sourisseau, J.-C. (eds) *Les Etrusques en mer : épaves d'Antibes à Marseille*. Aix-en-Provence, pgs. 25-31.

Long, L., Miro, J., Volpe, G. 1992. "Les épaves archaïques de la pointe Lequin (Porquerolles, Hyères, Var). Des données nouvelles sur le commerce de Marseille à la fin du Vie s. et dans la première moitié du Ve s. av. J.-C.," in Bats, M., Bertucchi, G., Congès, G., and Tréziny, H. (eds.),Marseille grecque et la Gaule (études Massaliètes 3), ADAM Editions, Lattes, pp. 199-234.

Long, L., Pomey, P. et Sourisseau, J.-C. (eds). 2002. *Les Etrusques en mer : épaves d'Antibes à Marseille*. Aix-en-Provence.

Loughton, M. 2003. "The distribution of Republican amphorae in France." *Oxford Journal of Archaeology* 22 (2), pgs. 177-207.

Louis, M. et al. 1958. *Le premier age du fer Languedocien*. Montpellier.

Lucan. *Pharsalia*. Penguin 1956.

Lüscher, G. 1996. "Der Amphorenimport in Châtillon-sur-Glâne (Kanton Freiburg / Schweiz)." *Germania* 74, pgs. 337-360.

Maggetti, M. and Schwab, H. 1982. "Iron Age fine pottery from Châtillon-sur-Glâne and the Heuneberg," *Archaeometry* 24 (1), pgs. 21-36.

Marnival, P. 1988. *L'alimentation végétale en France du Mésolithique jusqu'à l'âge du Fer*. CNRS, Paris.

Martin, R. 1965. *Manuel d'architecture grecque*. Paris.

Mattingly, D. 2007. *An imperial possession: Britain in the Roman Empire*. London.

Mauné, S., and Chazelles, C.-A. "Dynamique du peuplement et occupation du sol sur le territoire de Montlaurès (Narbonne, Aude)," in Clavel-Lévêque, M. and Vignot, A. (eds) *Cité et territoire II. Actes du IIe Colloque européen de Béziers (24-26 octobre 1997)*. Paris, pgs. 187-208.

Maxwell-Hyslop, K.R. 1971. *Western Asiatic Jewellery c. 3000-312 BC*. London.

Megaw, J.V.S. 1970. *Art of the European Iron Age: a study of the elusive image*. Bath.

Megaw, J.V.S. 1966. "The Vix burial," *Antiquity* 40, pgs. 38-44.

Megaw, V., and Megaw, R. 1995. "The Nature and Function of Celtic Art," in Miranda Green (ed), *The Celtic World*. London, 345-375.

Megaw, V., and Megaw, R. 1989. *Celtic Art: from its beginnings to the Book of Kells*. London.

Mela, Pomponius. *De situ orbis, libri tres*. Editio altera Etona 1789.

Michelozzi, A. 1982. *L'habitation protohistorique en Languedoc Oriental*. Association pour la Recherche Archéologique en Languedoc Oriental, Cahier 10, Caveirac.

Milcent, P.-Y. 2002. "Les importations étrusuqes dans le sud du Massif Central." Conference paper at the XXIV Covegno di Studi Etruschi e Italici, *Gli Etruschi da Genova ad Ampurias (VII-IV secolo A.C.)*. Marseille-Lattes 26 September- 1 October 2002.

Michel, R. H., McGovern, P. E., and Badler, V. R. 1992. "Chemical evidence for ancient beer." *Science* 360, pg. 24.

Millet, M. 1990. *The Romanization of Britain. An essay in archaeological interpretation*. Cambridge.

Moliner, M. 1996. "Marseille: Quartier du Panier, place des Pistoles." *Bilan Scientifique 1995, Direction Régionale des Affaires Culturelles, Service Régional de l'Archéologie, Provence-Alpes-Côte d'Azur*, pgs. 162–164.

Moliner, M. 1994. "Dispositifs de couverture et de signalisation dans la nécropole grecque de Sainte-Barbe à Marseille." *Documents d'Archéologie Méridonale* 17, pgs. 74–92.

Moliner, M., Mellinand, P., Naggiar, L. 2004. *La nécropolie de Sainte-Barbe à Massalia (IVe siècle av. J.-C. – IIe siècle ap. J.-C.) (etudes Massaliètes 8)*.

Momigliano, A. 1975. *Alien wisdom: The limits of Hellenization*. London.

Morel, J.-P. 1995. "Les Grecs et la Gaule," in *Les Grecs et l'Occident. Actes du Colloque de la Villa "Kérylos" (1991)*, école Française de Rome, Rome, pgs. 41–69.

Morel, J.P. 1990. "Les échanges entre la Grand-Grèce et la Gaule di VIIe au Ier siècle avant J.-C., » in Stazio, A. (ed) *La Magna Grecia e il lontano Occidente : atti del ventinovesimo Convegno di studi sulla Magna Greci : Taranto 6-11 ottobre 1989*. Toronto, pgs. 247-293.

Morel, J.-P. 1978. "A propos des céramiques campaniennes de France et d'Espagne." *Archeologie en Languedoc* I, pgs. 149-168.

Morel, J.-P. 1975. "L'expansion phocéenne en Occident : dix années de recherches (1966-1975)." *Bulletin de correspondance hellénique* 2, pgs. 853-896.

Morel, J.-P. 1969. "L' atelier des petites estampilles." MEFRA 80, pgs. 59-117.

Morhange, C., Laborel, J., Hesnard, A., Prone, A. 1996. "Variation of relative mean sea level during the last 4000 years on the northern shores of Lacydon, the ancient harbour ot Marseilles (Chantier J. Verne)." *Journal of Coastal Research* 12, pgs. 841-849.

Morhange, C., Hesnard, A., Laborel, J., and Prone, A. 1995. "Déplacement des lignes de rivage et mobilité du plan d'eau sur la rive nord du Lacydon de Marseille." *Méditerranée* 82(3.4), pgs. 71–76.

Murray, A.S. 2004. *A history of Greek sculpture*. London.

Nash, D. 2003. "Metals, salt, and slaves: economic links between Gaul and Italy from the eight to the late sixth centuries BC," *Oxford Journal of Archaeology* 22 (3), pgs. 243-259.

Nash, D. 1985. "Celtic territorial expansion and the Mediterranean World," in Champion, T.S. and Megaw, J.V.S. (eds) *Settlement and society. Aspects of West European prehistory in the first millennium BC*. Leicester, pgs. 45-68.

De Navarro, J.M. 1928. "Massilia and Early Celtic culture," *Antiquity* 2 (8), pgs. 423-442.

Nickels, A. 1989. "La Monédière à Bessan (Hérault). Le bilan des recherches." *Documents d'Archéologie Méridionale* 12, pgs. 51–120.

Nickels, A. 1983. "Les Grecs en Gaule: l'example du Languedoc," in *Modes de contacts et processus de transformation dans les sociétés anciennes*, école Française de Rome, Rome, pgs. 409–428.

Nickels, A. 1982. "Agde grecque, les recherches récentes." *La Parola del Passato* 204–207, pgs. 269–279.

Nickels, A. 1981. "Recherches sur la topographie de la ville antique d'Agde (Hérault)." *Documents d'Archéologie Méridionale* 4, pgs. 29–50.

Nickels, A. 1980. "Les plats à marli en céramique grise monochrome de type roussillonnais," in Barruol, G. (ed) *Ruscino. Chateau-Roussillon, Perpignan (Pyrénées-Orientales), I-état de travaux et recherches en 1975*. Paris, pgs. 155–162.

Nickels, A. 1978. "Contribution à l'étude de la céramique grise archaïque en Languedoc Roussillon," in Vallet, G. (ed) *Les céramiques de la Grèce de l'Est et leur diffusion en Occident (Actes du Colloque International du CNRS, 569, Naples, 1976)*. Bibliothèque de l'Institut Français de Naples, Naples, pgs. 248–267.

Nickels, A. 1976. "Les maisons à apside d'epoque grecque archaïque de la La Monédière à Bessan (Hérault)." *Gallia* 34, pgs. 95-128.

Nickels, A. Pellecuer, C., and Raynaud, C. 1981. "La necropole du 1er age du fer d'Agde: les tombes à importations grecques." MEFRA, pgs. 89-125.

Nicolini, G. 1995. "Gold wire techniques of Europe and the Mediterranean around 300 BC," in Morteani, G., and Northover, J. *Prehistoric gold in Europ: Mines, Metallurgy, and Manufacture*. Dordecht, pgs. 453-470.

Nicols, J. 1987. "Indigenous culture and the process of Romanization in Iberian Galicia," *American Journal of Philology* 108, pgs. 129-151.

Panosa Domingo, I. 1993. "Approche comparée de l'écriture ibérique en Languedoc-Roussillon et en Catalogne." *Documents d'Archéologie Méridionale* 16, pgs. 93–103.

Paret, O. 1952. "Das riche späthallstattzeitliche Grab con Schöckingen," *Fundberichte aus Schwaben* NF 12, pgs. 37-40.

Paret, O. 1938a. "Ein zweites Fürstengrab der Hallstattzeit von Stuttgart-Bad Cannstatt," *Fundberichte aus Schwaben* NF 9, pgs. 55-60.

Paret, O. 1938b. "Das Hallstattgrab von Sirnau bei Esslingen," *Fundberichte aus Schwaben* NF 9, pgs. 246-252.

Paret, O. 1935. "Das Fürstengrab der Hallstattzeit von Bad Cannstatt," *Fundberischte aus Schwaben* NF 8, Appendix I.

Pausanius. *Description of Greece: Attica and Corinth, books 1 and 2*. Loeb Classical Library, 1989.

Pearce, S. 1981. *The archeaology of south-west Britain*. London.

Penhallurick, R.D. 1986. *Tin in antiquity*. London.

Pétrequin, P., Louis, C., and Piningre, J.-J. 1985. *La grotte des Planches-près-Arbois (Jura)*. Paris.

Picon, M. 1985. "A propos de l'origine des amphores massaliètes: méthodes et résultats." *Documents d'Archéologie Méridionale* 8, pgs. 119–131.

Planchais, N. 1982. "Palynologie lagunaire de l'étang de Mauguio: paléoenvironment végétale et évolution anthropique." *Pollen and Spores* 24, pgs. 93-118.

Pliny the Elder. *Natural history*. Translation by H. Rackham, Harvard Univeristy Press 1989.

Plutarch. *Plutarch's Lives*. Translation by B. Perrin. Harvard University Press 1914-1926.

Pobé, M. and Roubier, J. 1961. *The Art of Roman Gaul: A Thousand Years of Celtic Art & Culture*. London.

Pomey, P., and Hesnard, A. 1993. "Les épaves romaines et grecques," in *Le temps des découvertes. Marseille de Protis à la reine Jeanne*, Marseille, pgs. 59–62.

Pournod, J. 1990. "Auriol," in Arcelin, P. (ed) *Voyage en Massalie. 100 ans d'archaéologie en Gaule du Sud (Marseille)*, pgs. 146-153.

Powell, T.G.E. 1958. *The Celts*. London.

Prades, H., and Groupe Archéologique Painlevé (eds). 1985. *L'occupation des rivages de l'Etang de Mauguio (Hérault) au Bronze Final et au Premier Age du Fer, Vol. I*. Association poir la Recherche Archéologique en Languedoc Oriental, Cahier 11, Caveirac.

Py, M. 1996a. "Les maisons protohistoriques de Lattara (Ive-Ier s. av. n.è.), approche typologique et fonctionelle," in Py, M. (ed) *Lattara 9: Urbanisme et architecture dans la ville antique de Lattes*. Lattes, pgs. 141-258.

Py, M. (ed). 1996b. *Lattara 9: Urbanisme et architecture dans la ville antique de Lattes*. Lattes.

Py, M. 1993a. *Les Gaulois du Midi: de la fin de l'Age du Bronze à la conquête romaine*. Paris.

Py, M. 1993b. "Céramique à pâte claire héraultaise," in Py, M. (ed) *Lattara 6: DICOCER. Dictionnaire des céramiques antiques (VIIe s. av. n.è.-VIIe s. de n.è.) en Méditerranée nord-occidentale (Provence, Languedoc, Ampurdan)*, ARALO, Lattes, pgs. 204–205.

Py, M. 1993c. "Céramique grise monochrome," in Py, M. (ed) *Lattara 6: DICOCER. Dictionnaire des céramiques antiques (VIIe s. av. n.è.-VIIe s. de n.è.) en Méditerranée nord-occidentale (Provence, Languedoc, Ampurdan)*, ARALO, Lattes, pgs. 445–452.

Py, M. 1993d. "Céramique pseudo-attique massaliète," in Py, M. (ed) *Lattara 6: DICOCER. Dictionnaire des céramiques antiques (VIIe s. av. n.è.-VIIe s. de n.è.) en Méditerranée nord-occidentale (Provence, Languedoc, Ampurdan)*, ARALO, Lattes, pgs. 536–538.

Py, M. 1990a. "Espeyran," in Arcelin, P. (ed) *Voyage en Massalie : 100 ans d'archéologie en Gaule du Sud*. Marseille, pgs. 190-193.

Py, M. 1990b. *Culture, économie et société protohistoriques dans la région nimoise* (2 vols.), école Française de Rome, Rome.

Py, M. (ed). 1990c. *Lattara 3: Fouilles dans la ville antique de Lattes. Les îlots 1, 3, et 4-nord du quartier Saint-Sauveur*. Lattes.

Py, M. (ed). 1989. *Lattara 2: Introduction à létude de l'environnement de Lattes antique*. Lattes.

Py, M. 1978a. "Quatre siècles d'amphore massaliète, essai de classification des bords." *Figlina* 3, pgs. 1–23.

Py, M. 1978b. "Une production massaliète de céramique pseudo-attique à vernis noir," *Revue d'études Ligures* 44, pgs. 175–198.

Py, M. 1978c. *L'oppidum des Castels à Nages, Gard, fouilles 1958–1978*. Gallia Supplement 35, Paris.

Py, M. 1976. "Note sur l'évolution des céramiques à vernis noir des oppida languedociens de Roque de Viou et de Nages, Gard." MEFRA 88, pgs. 545-606.

Py, M. 1971. "La céramique grecque de Vaunage (Gard) et sa signification." *Cahiers Ligures de Préhistoire et d'Archéologie* 20, pgs. 5–153.

Py, M. and Buxó i Capdevila, R. 2001. "La viticulture en Gaule à l'âge du fer." *Gallia* 58, pgs. 29-41.

Py, F. and M. Py. 1974. "Les amphores etrusques de Vaunage et de Villevieille, Gard." MEFRA 86, pgs. 141-254.

Rapoport, A. 1969. *House Form and Culture*. Englewood Cliffs.

Rasmussen, T. B. 2006. *Bucchero pottery from southern Etruria*. Cambridge.

Reille, J.-L. 2001. "L'importation des meules domestiques dans la forteresse grecque d'Olbia (Hyères, Var) entre le IIe s. av. n. è. et le Haut Empire." *Documents d'Archéologie méridionale* 24, pgs. 207-211.

Reille, J. L. 1985. "L'analyse pétrographique des céramiques et le problème de la provenance des amphores massaliètes (VIème-IIème s. av. J.-C.)." *Documents d'Archéologie Méridionale* 8, pgs. 101–112.

Reille, J.-L., and Abbas, G. 1992. "Les inclusions minérales des amphores massaliètes et leur signification: le cas des formes archaïques et le problème de la localisation des sites de production." *Documents d'Archéologie Méridionale* 15, pgs. 431–437.

Richard, J.-C. 1992. "La diffusion des monnayages massaliètes au-delà du territoire de Marseille," in Bats, M., Bertucchi, G., Congès, G., and Tréziny, H. (ed.) *Marseille grecque et la Gaule (études Massaliètes 3)*, Lattes, pgs. 255–260.

Richard, J.-C. 1990. "Les monnaies du Midi de la Gaule," in Duval, A., Morel, J. P., and Roman, Y. (eds) *Gaule interne et Gaule méditerranéenne aux IIe et Ier siècles avant J.-C.: confrontations chronologiques*. CNRS, Revue Archéologique de Narbonnaise Supplement 21, Paris, pgs. 37–38.

Richard, J.-C., and Villaronga, L. 1973. "Recherches sur les étalons monétaires en Espagne et en Gaule du Sud antérieurement à l'époque d'Auguste." *Mélanges de la Casa Velasquez* 9, pgs. 81–131.

Richarté, C., Richier, A., and Sauzade, G. 1995. *Marseille: Palais du Pharo.Bilan Scientifique 1994*, Direction Régionale des Affaires Culturelles, Service Régional de l'Archéologie, Provence-Alpes-Côte d'Azur, pgs. 140–144.

Riffaud, P. 1989. *Prospection et inventaire des vestiges archéologiques aux abords du sité de Glanum*. Aix-en-Provence.

Ricq-De Bouard, M. 1985. "Le problème de l'origine des amphores massaliètes. Comparison pétrographique et minéralogique de tessons venant des sites d'Olbia et d'Espeyran, des ateliers marseillais de la Butte des Cannes et de Velaux." *Documents d'Archéologie Méridionale* 8, pgs. 113–117.

Rivet, A. L. F. 1988. *Gallia Narbonensis: Southern Gaul in Roman Times*. London.

Rolland, H. 1960. "Trouvaille d'Entremont." *Rev. Num.* ser. 6. II, pgs. 37-51.

Rolland, H. 1958. *Fouilles de Glanum 1947-1956*. Paris.

Rolland, H. 1956. *Fouilles de Saint-Blaise 1951-1956*. Gallia Supplement VII.

Rolland, H. 1951. *Fouilles de Saint-Blaise (Bouches-du-Rhône)*. Gallia Supplement III. Paris.

Rolland, H. 1949. "L'expansion du monnayage de Marseille dans le pays celto-ligure." *RSL* XV, pgs. 139-148.

Rolland, H. 1946. *Fouilles de Glanum (Saint-Rémy de Provence)*. Gallia Supplement 1. Paris.

Rolland, H. 1936. *Fouilles d'un habitat préromain à Saint-Remy de Provence*. Marseille.

Rolland, H. 1935. "Sur les drachmes lourdes de Massalia." *Provincia* 15, pgs. 231-246.

Rolley, C. 1962. "Trouvailles méditerranéennes en Basse-Bourgogne," *Bulletin de Correspondance Hellénique* 86 (livraison II), pgs. 476-493.

Rosen-Przeworska, J. 1964a. "Some Celtic-Scythian parallels," *Archaeologia Polona* 6, pgs. 65-105.

Rosen-Przeworska, J. 1964b. *Tradycje Celtyckie w obrzędowości protosłowian*. Warsaw.

Roth Congès, A. 2000. *Glanum. De l'oppidum salyen à la*

cité romaine. Paris.

Roth Congès, A. 1997. "La fortune éphémère de Glanum: du religieux à l'économique," *Gallia* 54, pgs. 157-200.

Roth Congès, A. 1992a. "Le centre monumental de Glanon, ou les derniers deux de la civilisation salyenne," in Bats, M., Bertucchi, G., Congès, G., and Tréziny, H. (eds) *Marseille grecque et la Gaule (Études Massaliètes 3)*. Lattes, pgs. 351-367.

Roth Congès, A. 1992b. "Monuments publics d'époque tardo-hellénistique à Glanon (B.-du-Rh.)," *Documents d'Archéologiie Méridionale* 15, pgs. 50-56.

Roth Congès, A. 1992c. "Nouvelles fouilles à Glanum (1982-1990)," *Journal of Roman Archaeology* 5, pgs. 39-55.

Rothenberg, B. and Blanco-Freijerio, A. 1981. *Ancient Mining and Metallurgy in South-West Spain*. Institute for Archeo-Metallurgical Studies.

Rotroff, S.I. 1978. "Athenian pottery: 'Megarian bowls.'" *Current Anthropology* 19 (2), pgs. 387-388.

Rouillard, P. 1992. "La place de Marseille dans le commerce des vases attiques à figures rouges en Méditerranée occidentale (Ve-IVe sièces avant J.-C.) dans Marseille grecque et la Gaule," Etudes Massaliètes 3, pgs.179-187.

Ruas, M.P. 1989. "Étude carpologique," in Fiches, J.L. (ed) *L'oppidum d'Ambrussum et son territoire, fouilles au quatier du Sablas (Villetelle, Hérault) 1979-1985*. Monographie du Centre Recherches Archéologiques 2, pgs. 169-180.

Sanders, N.K. 1957. *Bronze Age cultures in France: the later phases from the thirteenth to the seventh century B.C.* Cambrige.

Schaff, U. 1969. "Versuch einer regionalen Gliederung frühlatènezeitlicher Fürstengräber," *Fundber. Aus Hessen.*, pgs. 187-202.

Schwab, H. 1982. "Pseudophokäische und Phokäische Keramik in Châtillon-sur-Glâne."*Archäologisches Korrespondenzblatt* 12, pgs. 363-372.

Schwaller, M. 1991. "The settlement and cemetery at Ensérune," in Moscati, et. al (eds) *The Celts*. New York, pgs. 349-355.

Scotto, R.-F. 1985. "La céramique grise à décor ondé de Montmorot (Jura)," in Bonnamour, L., Duval, A., and Guillaumet, J.-P. (eds) *Les Ages du Fer dans la vallée de la SaÔne (VIIe-Ier siècles avant notre ère). Paléométallurgie du bronze à l'Age du Fer (Actes du VIIe Colloque de l'A.F.E.A.F. tenu à Rully, 12–15 mai 1983)*. CNRS, Revue Archéoloqique de l'Est et du Centre-Est Supplement 6, Paris, pgs. 45–51.

Shefton, B.B. 1989. "Zun import and einfluss mediterraner Güter in Alteuropa," *Kölner Jahrbuch für Vor- und Frühgeschichte* 22, pgs. 207-220.

Shefton, B.B. 1979. *Die 'rhodischen' Bronzekannen*. Mainz.

Snodgrass, A.M. 2001. "Pausanias and the Chest of Kypselos," in Alcock, S., Cherry, J., and Elsner, J. (eds) *Pausanias. Travel and memory in Roman Greece*. Oxford, pgs. 127-141.

Snodgrass, A.M. 1998. *Homer and the artists text and picture in early Greek art*. London.

Solier, Y. 1976–1978. "La culture ibéro-languedocienne aux VIe-Ve siècles." *Ampurias* 38–40, pgs. 211–264.

Sourisseau, J.-Chr. 1990. *Les amphores du Jardin d'Hiver à Arles (B.-du-Rh.): étude dynamique de ces conteneurs commerciaux*. Université de Provence, 1990.

Strabo. *Geography, books 1-14*. Translation by H.L. Jones, Harvard Loeb 1989.

Tacitus. *The Complete Works*. McGraw-Hill Higher Education, 1965.

Taffanel, O. and Taffanel, J. 1960. "Deux tombes de chef a Mailhac." *Gallia* 18, pgs. 1-37.

Taffanel, O., Taffanel, J., and Richard, J.-C. 1979. "Les monnaies de Mailhac (Aude) (1931-1977)." *Gallia* 37, pgs. 1-53.

Taylor, T. 2001. "Believing the ancients: quantitative and qualitative dimensions of slavery and the slave trade in later prehistoric Eurasia," *World Archaeology* 33, pgs. 27-43.

Terral, J.-F.1997. *Domestication de l'olivier (Olea europaea) en Mediterranée nord-occidentale: approche morphométrique et implications paléoclimatiques*. Doctoral Thesis, University of Montpellier II.

Terral, J.F., Alonso, N., Buxo i Capdevila, R., Chatti, N., Fabre, L., Fiorentino, G., Marinval, P., Jorda, G.P., Pradat, B., Rovira, N., and Alibert, P. 2004. "Historical biogeography of olive domestication (Olea europaea L.) as revealed by geometrical morphometry applied to biological and archaeological material." *Journal of Biogeography* 31, pgs. 63-77.

Tchernia, A. 1983. "Italian wine in Gaul at the end of the Republic," in Garnsey, P., Hopkins, K., Whittaker, C.R. (eds) *Trade in the ancient economy*. London, pgs. 87-104.

Thucydides. *History IV 1 – V.24*. Translation by P.J. Rhodes, Aris and Phillips 1998.

Treister, M.Y. 1997. *The role of metals in ancient Greek history*. Leiden.

Tréziny, H. 1995. "La topographie de Marseille antique de sa fondation (600 av. J.-C.) à l'époque romaine." *Méditerranée* 82(3.4), pgs. 41–52.

Tréziny, H. 1992. "Imitations, emprunts, détournements : sur quelques problèmes d'architecture et d'urbanisme en Gaule méridionale," in Bats, M., Bertucchi, G., Congès, G., and Tréziny, H. (eds) *Marseille grecque et la Gaule (études Massaliètes 3)*, Lattes, pgs. 337-349.

Tréziny, H. 1985. "Remarques sur la fonction du rampart hellénistique de Saint-Blaise," in Bats, M., and Tréziny, H. (eds) *Le territoire de Marseille grecque (études Massaliètes 1)*. Aix-en-Provence, pgs. 145-151.

Tréziny, H., and Trousset, P. 1992. "Les fortifications de Marseille grecque," in Bats, M., Bertucchi, G., Congès, G., and Tréziny, H. (eds) *Marseille grecque et la Gaule (études Massaliètes 3)*, Lattes, pgs. 89–107.

Uenze, H.P. 1964. "Zur Frühlatènezeit in der Oberpfalz," *Bayer. Vorgeschichtsbl.* 29, pgs. 77-118.

Ugolini, D., and Olive, C. 1987–1988. "Un four de potier du Ve s. av. J.-C. à Béziers, Place de la Madeleine." *Gallia* 45, pgs. 13–28.

Van Arsdell, R. D. 1989. *Celtic coinage of Britain*. London.

Vasseur, G. 1914. *L'origine de Marseille. Fondations des premiers comptoirs ioniens de Massalia vers le milieu du VIIe siècle. Résultats de fouilles archéologique exécutées à Marseille dans le Fort Saint-Jean.,* Moullot Fils Aîné (Annales du Musée d'Histoire Naturelle de Marseille

13), Marseille.

Verdin, F., Brien-Poitevin, Fr., Chabal, L., Marinval, P., and Provansal, M. 1996-1997. "Coudounèu (Lançon-de-Provence, Bouches-du-Rhône) : une ferme-grenier et son terroir au Ve s. av. J.-C." *DAM* 19-20, pgs. 165-198.

Villard, F. 1960. *La céramique greque de Marseille*. Paris.

Villaronga, L. 1986. "Imitacions gàlliques de les dracmes de Rhode i Empòrion." *Acta numismatica* 16, pgs. 21-51.

Virgil. *Aenid*. Translation by W.F. Jackson Knight, Penguin 1976.

von Massow, W. 1916. "Die Cypseluslade," *Ath. Mitt.* 41, pgs. 1-117.

Wallon, D. 1979. "Les cols d'amphores "massaliètes" ; de l'oppidum de Montjean (La Môle, Var)." *Revue Archéologique de Narbonnaise* 12, pgs. 43–54.

Wells, P. 1985. "Mediterranean trade and culture change in Early Iron Age central Europe," in Champion, T.S. and Megaw, J.V.S. (eds) *Settlement and society. Aspects of West European prehistory in the first millennium BC*. Leicester, pgs. 69-90.

Wells, P. 1984. *Farms, villages, and cities: commerce and urban origins in Late Prehistoric Europe*. Ithica.

Wells, P. 1980. *Culture contact and culture change: Early Iron Age Central Europe and the Mediterranean World*. Cambridge.

Willaume, M. 1985. *Le Berry à l'Âge du Fer, HaC-La Tène II*. Oxford BAR International Series 247.

Wiseman, J. 1998. "Insight: a visit to ancient Glanum," *Archaeology* 51 (6), pgs. 12-18.

Woolf, G. 1998. *Becoming Roman. The origins of provincial civilization in Gaul*. Cambridge.

Woolf, G. 1997. "Beyond Romans and natives." *World Archaeology* 28 (3), pgs. 339-350.

Zürn, H. 1970. *Hallstattforschungen in Nordwürttenberg*. Stuttgart.

www.ingramcontent.com/pod-product-compliance
Lightning Source LLC
Chambersburg PA
CBHW061550010526
44115CB00023B/2997